FRÄULEIN TOMM-TOMM

FRÄULEIN TOMM-TOMM

Ursula Atkins

*To my friend Coral
with best wishes
from Ursula*

20.2.1997

The Book Guild Ltd
Sussex, England

The Book Guild Ltd
25 High Street
Lewes, Sussex

First published 1997
© Ursula Atkins 1997
Set in Times
Typesetting by Southern Reproductions (Sussex)
Crowborough, Sussex
Printed in Great Britain by
Bookcraft (Bath) Ltd, Avon

A catalogue record for this book is
available from the British Library

ISBN 1 85776 152 9

In loving memory of
my mother and father

ACKNOWLEDGEMENTS

I would like to express my appreciation for the encouragement that I have received from my family and friends which led to the writing of this book.

In particular, I would like to thank Tracey Parker for allowing me to reproduce her two splendid drawings.

Special thanks also go to my husband, Fred, for his suggestions and help in all the stages of my book's preparation.

INTRODUCTION

Life for our family Kaeding in the Eilbek district of Hamburg in 1939 was like that of any other ordinary German family. My father, Otto, worked in the Meteorological office in Hamburg and my mother, Margarethe, followed the usual pattern of that time, being a full-time housewife and mother to me, aged three, and my brother, Richard, aged one.

The outbreak of war led to the call-up of my father and his brother, Arnold (who was killed in action), into the army and to the difficulties experienced by the rest of the family in the wake of the allied bombing of Hamburg.

Countless memories of the following years remain to me as vivid today as they ever were, and these form the basis of this book.

1

Two things I will hate for the rest of my life are the sounds of wailing sirens and the deep drone of heavy Lancaster bombers. They bring back memories of World War II, which ended 50 years ago.

I was lucky not having to experience the firestorm in Hamburg towards the end of July 1943; but my mother and my five-year-old brother Richard went through it and survived. Leading up to it, the bombing intensified, and many children were evacuated.

On the thirteenth of July 1943, just before my seventh birthday, I found myself with hundreds of other children standing on a platform at our main railway station in Hamburg, waiting for the train to take us away to a place considered to be safer from the bombings. My mother told me that I was too skinny, and a holiday near the seaside would do me good. I accepted that explanation. I only wondered why I had to go, though my brother, who was two years younger than me, could stay at home with my mother.

Home was a flat in a three-storey house at 30b Rossberg (horse mountain) in Eilbek, a densely populated residential area in Hamburg. At the end of the road was our school, where I started in the autumn of 1942. It was, and still is, the custom in Germany to sweeten the start of school with a *Schultüte*, a cone-shaped sweet bag which was quite often nearly as tall as the child. I felt really disappointed that I did not receive one, but my mother promised me a plateful of sweets when I came out of school, which I was very much looking forward to.

There were rows of wooden desks with inkwells on top, an enormous blackboard at the front, and a middle-aged teacher who sat at a single huge desk in front of us. When I look back now, it occurs to me that all my teachers seemed to have been middle-aged during my school time. We learned to write with a dip-pen and ink, in joined-up writing. Every day I came home with ink-stained fingers, and my exercise books did not look any better. Our school day started at 8.00 a.m. and finished at lunchtime.

Next to the school were underground air-raid shelters with thick concrete walls and rows of bunkbeds with itchy grey blankets. It became a way of life being woken up by the sound of sirens and my mother, and getting dressed quickly in our little square hall. The picture of Reichs-President Paul von Hindenburg with his grey moustache and solemn face always looked down on us. How I hated the liberty bodice (it was so fiddly getting the woolly stockings attached to it), helping Richard to get dressed and rushing down from the first-floor flat out onto the path between the front gardens of the ground-floor flats, through the archway with the flats above and where the dustbins stood, and onto the pavement of our street.

I particularly remember one occasion, when it was bitterly cold and the snow was pushed into big heaps against the pavement from the road. We had to cross the road to get to the shelter. My poor mother, who was pushing us along, did not see the piled-up snow in her haste and fell right across it, ripping her silk stockings. However, she still managed to hold on to us, and her little case in which she kept just our papers, some family photographs and a small box of jewellery. In the end, that was all that remained when we lost our home in the second saturation bombing night by the Royal Air Force, the twenty-eighth of July 1943, when the heavens opened with phosphorus, incendiary bombs and blockbusters, killing 40,000, mostly ordinary civilians, including 3,500 children.

I have some lovely memories of an elderly couple, Mr and Mrs Hildebrandt, who lived on the same floor as us. They always called me Fräulein Tomm-Tomm. I could not pronounce the K of *Komm, Komm* (come, come) when I started to talk. I used to sit on a little low stool in their small kitchen and knew exactly where they kept the sugar lumps in their dresser.

On each floor was a bucket of sand. Mr and Mrs Hildebrandt were often on air-raid duties and stayed behind when we rushed to the shelter. We later heard that they had to use a saw to get through the wrought-iron fencing in the back so that they could escape. Mrs Hildebrandt died not long afterwards, perhaps due to that air raid.

I also remember Gerd Danschke, a slightly older boy who lived on the second or third floor. I often wondered what happened to him. There were children everywhere, and we played games in the forecourt, like blind man's buff, skipping, sleeping beauty, marbles and hiding. The family on the ground floor occasionally let us play in their front garden, but Richard spoiled the fun, piercing my colourful ball on the spikes of the wrought-iron fencing. Always being inquisitive, I quite often inspected the dustbins, lifting up the lids to look at the contents. What a smell! Once I found some quite nice-looking stalks of rhubarb. I did not mind the sharp taste when sucking one of them, only being interrupted and told off by my mother, who had come rushing out, after a neighbour told her what I was doing. It seems that the idea of 'Neighbourhood Watch' was invented many years ago.

The dairy shop was right at the corner next to the archway. It was always very cool with its white-and-blue-tiled walls and smelled clean and fresh. The milk was stored in big metal churns and ladled out into the metal milk can that we brought along. A big lump of butter lay on a marbled table, and I was fascinated to watch the lady patting a piece with two wooden spatulas over and over again until it had the required shape and weight to be wrapped up in waxed greaseproof paper for the customer.

To the back of the shop was the storeroom. We had heard that a cat and her kittens had their home there in a cardboard box. Richard and I sneaked in to have a look and to stroke the balls of fluff. The protective mother bit me, so we never went near them again.

The winter of 1942–43 was very cold, and we had plenty of snow. Central heating was unknown to us in those days. After getting up in the mornings we looked at the lovely icy patterns on the window panes in the kitchen. My mother had to prise the dark blanket off the kitchen window sill, put there to keep out the cold. There was a blackout every evening, and we used dark-green roller blinds. No light was allowed to escape to attract the bombers. Every evening a man patrolled along the path at the back of the houses and shouted up to anybody who let a flicker of light escape from their windows.

My mother let us play out until it was dark. It was a safe road with hardly any traffic. One day, hordes of children made a long slide. It was great fun, and we often ended up on our bottoms. We came home absolutely soaked and freezing. My feet were like lumps of ice, and little puddles formed when we stood in the hall, waiting for my mother to pull off our black bootees. Our kitchen was small but cosy, with the hot kitchen range in the corner to the right of the window. My mother set me in front of it, and I put my frozen feet as far as I dared into the open oven. It was also used for heating up bricks, which Richard and I had wrapped up in newspaper and an old piece of blanket at the bottom of our beds. This was our equivalent of a hot-water bottle.

The Saturday night cleaning sessions were great fun for us. We had no bathroom, just a toilet. My mother kept a small zinc bath with a handle at each end in the little storeroom, which we could reach via a door from the kitchen, at the left-hand side of the window. First it was my brother's turn to be lifted into the warm water. I was next and could stay in a little bit longer, searching for the slippery soap and splashing the kitchen floor, while my mother saw to my brother, dressing him into freshly laundered night-clothes. It was always lovely and warm sitting in front of the kitchen range during the winter months. During the summer my mother used a small electric cooker with two hotplates.

The kitchen was also my playground on rainy days. I possessed a small doll's house with a little stove in it, a set of tiny aluminium saucepans, and my mother lit a night light in the stove for cooking. I loved colourful balls, but a small kitchen was not the right place to throw them about. They always landed on the hot kitchen range and were burned, giving off the most dreadful smell. My other favourite pastime was washing my dolls' clothes. Because of lack of space, I was allowed to attach one end of the washing line to a handle on the dresser and the other to the kitchen door handle, which meant I had to hold the line with the pegged washing in one hand when my mother wanted to leave the kitchen. Our little coal bunker in the kitchen was always an attraction to us. We often ended up with black hands, pulling the coal out of the little door at the bottom, when we were just about to go out. I remember the glass potty I used in the toilet suddenly breaking, and sitting on the cold linoleum floor amongst the debris. My mother was more concerned about cuts than the mess on the floor. But she was amazed when I did not suffer a single scratch.

Once, two of the neighbourhood's children sent me to the little corner shop at the other side of the archway to buy a pennyworth of *Hau mi blau* (smack me blue). I was very hesitant and kept asking what sort of sweets they were. When I went into the shop I lingered about, but did not have the courage to ask and bought some *Salmi* (liquorice) instead. It was a sort of flat, diamond-shaped piece of liquorice, that you stuck onto the back of your hand and licked, ending up with a black tongue. This little shop was always an attraction to me, with its glass jars of sweets standing on shelves along the walls and on the counter. There were trays of *Butterkuchen* (yeast cake topped with flakes of butter) and *Streuselkuchen* (yeast cake topped with crumble), and also *Apfelkuchen* (apple cake) and *Berliners* (jam-filled doughnuts) in the far corner. On hot summer days all shops pulled out striped awnings, and the leafy trees kept the broad pavements partly in the shade. We received the occasional penny, which was either spent on sweets or on a piece of day-old cake.

Further along the road, Olly, an older girl, often sat on the front step of her flat. All children used to tease her because she was different, not quite right in the head, we always said. It was rather cruel, teasing a handicapped child, but we didn't know any better.

For a short while Richárd and I went to a day nursery along the Wandsbeker Chaussee. There we were supposed to take a nap after lunch, which we did not like very much, so we decided to walk home one afternoon. Nobody stopped us. My mother was amazed when she saw us turning into our road just as she was coming to collect us. That was the end of our nursery days.

I remember one December day when we visited our Aunt Trudel (Gertrude) and Uncle Fiete (Friedrich), who lived within walking distance in Wandsbek. I was nearly three and a half years old. My brother Richard was still in his pram and I was sitting on top of it on a wooden board with side panels, which my father had made. One of my two cousins, Gerd, was much older than me and went out with friends carol-singing in the neighbourhood. When he came back, he had his pockets and hands full of oranges, apples and sweets. I never knew there were so many pockets in a boy's coat and trousers.

Later in the evening after tea we left for home. My mother pushed the pram with my sleeping brother, and I hopped and skipped along the icy path, holding my father's hand. I was so excited, seeing all the stars on this clear freezing night. I never stopped asking about their names.

We always had plenty of snow each winter, and I loved white Christmases. Christmas 1939 was no exception. Richard and I had beautifully knitted woolly suits with matching hats as presents. Mine was light blue with navy blue spots and Richard's was navy blue with white spots. After dinner on Christmas Day my father brought the wooden sledge out from the cellar and sat us both on it, with

6

me leaning against the wrought-iron backing, holding on to my brother in front of me. My mother wrapped us both into a blanket and off we went to the Eichtal Park in Wandsbek, my father pulling the sledge and my mother walking next to us. I was fascinated by my mother's feet, which looked enormous as she was wearing overshoes with press studs on each side over her ordinary street shoes.

Enjoying the snow in the park, I proudly showed off my new suit. When we came back home, I did not want to take it off, even though I was cold and wet.

When I was about four years old, for reasons never explained to me, I stayed for a while at a children's home in Malente, a small town in the Holsteinische Schweiz (Swiss Holstein), the county north of Hamburg. The bedroom slept about six girls, and I had my bed next to the window. I had to wear thumbless cotton mittens during the night as I kept biting my nails. I never quite understood why I had to stay there, and I wanted to go home. When I eventually did come home after a few weeks, my mother was very pleased to see me and could not get over what a lovely tan I had. I was always pale, and the change of air had done me good.

One Christmas, the Christmas of 1942, I will not forget. On Christmas Eve Richard and I were dressed up, and I had an enormous *Butterlecker* (butter licker), a big white satin bow, in my hair. It was 4.00 p.m. We were waiting in our only bedroom, when the little brass Christmas bell rang. We rushed out and into the parlour, which was reserved for special occasions. There stood a lovely Christmas tree with all the white candles flickering and lighting up the dark room. There were beautiful glass baubles, chocolates, a couple of little trumpets we could blow and plenty of tinsel hanging from the tree. On the table underneath it we found a plate with oranges, nuts and a marzipan loaf for each of us. Suddenly the doorbell rang, and Father Christmas was let in by my mother. Richard hid behind my mother to start with and looked at him in anticipation. He wore a long red coat and had a white beard. From the sack he carried we saw the *Rute* (bundle of rods), which was for the naughty children. I

7

asked why Papa was not there, and my brother commented that Father Christmas wore his daddy's boots. But it never clicked!

We stood like little statues in front of the Christmas tree, saying our Christmas poems. My brother kept his poem short; after all, he was only four years old. He said:

Lieber, guter Weihnachtsmann,
> Dear, good Father Christmas.
Schau mich nicht so böse an,
> Look not angrily at me;
Steck die Rute wieder ein,
> Put away the *Rute*, then,
Ich will auch immer artig sein,
> And good I'll always be.

My poem, by Theodor Storm, was rather longer, and it took me weeks at school to memorise it:

Knecht Ruprecht

Von drauß', vom Walde komm ich her;
Ich muß euch sagen, es weihnachtet sehr!
Allüberall auf den Tannenspitzen
Sah ich goldene Lichtlein blitzen;
Und droben aus dem Himmelstor
Sah mit großen Augen das Christkind hervor.
Und wie ich so strolcht' durch den finstern Tann,
Da rief's mich mit heller Stimme an;
'Knecht Ruprecht' rief es, 'alter Gesell,
Hebe die Beine und spute dich schnell!
Die Kerzen fangen zu brennen an,
Das Himmelstor ist aufgetan,
Alt' und Junge sollen nun
Von der Jagd des Lebens einmal ruhn.
Und morgen flieg' ich hinab zur Erden,
Denn es soll wieder Weihnachten werden!

Ich sprach: 'O lieber Herre Christ,
Meine Reise fast zu Ende ist;
Ich soll nur noch in diese Stadt,
Wo's eitel gute Kinder hat.'
– 'Hast denn das Säcklein auch bei dir?'
Ich sprach: 'Das Säcklein, das ist hier;
Denn Äpfel, Nuß und Mandelkern
Essen fromme Kinder gern.'
– 'Hast denn die Rute auch bei dir?'
Ich sprach: 'Die Rute, die ist hier;
Doch für die Kinder nur, die schlechten,
Die trifft sie auf den Teil den rechten.'
Christkindlein sprach: 'So ist es recht;
So geh mit Gott, mein treuer Knecht!'
Von drauß', vom Walde komm ich her;
Ich muß euch sagen, es weihnachtet sehr!
Nun sprecht, wie ich's hierinnen find'!
Sind's gute Kind, sind's böse Kind?

Servant Ruprecht

From outside, from the woods I come
To tell that Christmas must be here
And everywhere, in pine tree tops,
Golden lights I see, a-sparkling;
And high above, from heaven's gates
Looked out, wide-eyed, the Christ-child.
And as through dark pines I strolled
He called to me with voice so clear;
'Servant Ruprecht, old fellow,' he called,
'Come along in haste!
The candles start to light,
The heavenly gates are open wide,
And old and young shall now
From life's toil rest awhile,
And tomorrow down to earth will I fly,
And once more Christmas will it be.'

'Oh, my dear Christ,' quoth I,
'My travels near their end,
I shall visit where, in this town,
Only good children are.'
'Have you your little sack with you?'
'The little sack is here,' I said,
'For apples, nuts and almonds by devout
                            children are eaten.'
'Do you have the *Rute* with you?'
'The *Rute* is here,' said I.
'But only for the bad children,
To beat a little sore.'
The Christ-child said, 'Thus all is right;
So go with God, my servant loyal!'
'From outside, from the woods, I come
To tell that Christmas must be here.
Then let me know, what find I here,
Are children good or are they bad?'

Only then could we receive our presents. Father Christmas reached deep into his sack and gave us games and some little toys. Under the Christmas tree I found a little wicker doll's pram with a sleeping cuddly doll in it, and Richard was delighted with his wooden castle and tin soldiers. My brother's godfather, Uncle Richard, came on Christmas morning to give us each a beautiful little accordion, but my mother said we were a little bit too small and put them into the big wall unit in the parlour.

I did not realise then that this was to be our last Christmas together in our flat as a family. We never learned to play the accordion, and we never saw Uncle Richard again. When I asked my mother where he was, she just could not answer me and looked very sad.

My father had by then been called up to serve in the army, and he was on leave that Christmas. I did not understand what war really meant, I only noticed my father was not there any more in the evenings after work, and I missed him.

My first experience with the theatre was a trip to a Christmas play with my mother, just after Christmas. It was held in a huge hall with very dim lights; the blackout was obeyed by everybody. They played *Hänsel and Gretel.* In one corner of the hall stood a huge stove. When Gretel asked the witch to see if the fire was really hot enough, somebody opened the door of the stove, and I could see a mountain of glowing coal. It looked enormous, and I was convinced that Gretel pushed the witch into it. All the children screamed, including me. It took my mother a long time to calm me down on the way home.

One rainy day my mother went to the corner shop and I decided to play hairdressers. I knew where the pair of scissors were, sat my brother on a chair in the kitchen and cut a lovely triangle out of his bushy fringe. My mother was not very amused when she came back and I showed her my masterpiece.

My brother was also skilled with his hands. From our bedroom a door led onto the balcony, which had nasturtiums in boxes flowering all around the railings. We had beautiful, lacy floor-length net curtains covering the balcony door. One evening, when my mother went to see a friend, we woke up and Richard decided to rummage through my father's stamp albums, which were kept in his bedside table, although I told him off. It was still light, and he decided to redesign the net curtains, using the scissors I had cut his hair with, and was cutting long strips upwards from the hem. Mrs Hildebrandt was supposed to pop in now and then to see if we were all right, but he was caught in the act by my mother. She and her friend had been watching our bedroom window from an opposite flat. I cannot remember if those curtains were ever repaired or replaced. A few weeks later they went up in flames anyway.

We did not go to school in the summer of 1943 after the Americans started bombing raids during the day. When the wail of the sirens sounded the All-Clear, we dashed out of the shelter and carried on playing the games we had stopped before the raid.

11

Coming out to play one morning, we found thousands of silver foil strips everywhere on the ground. We dashed around to pick up as many as we could, counting them, to see how many each child had. They were thrown out of the British air force bombers prior to their raids, to confuse the German radar, and were called by the code name Window.

Another episode I remember well; having just one bedroom for all four of us, it cannot have escaped my parents' attention that I snored. My mother took me to the doctor, and he said that my adenoids needed shortening. I was nervously sitting on a nurse's lap in front of the doctor in his surgery. My mother was in the waiting room next to it, and there was a small hatch in the connecting wall through which she could watch me. The doctor put a mask on my face, and that really set me off. I must have screamed down the whole building until it was all over.

The other time I had to see a doctor was to have a couple of stitches put into my hand. During one of his leaves, my father was mending the lock on our flat door when he dropped a nail. I was watching him and bent down to pick it up for him. He did not see me behind him, and stepped onto my hand with his nailed army boots. Luckily only the flesh between my right thumb and forefinger was pierced.

Only once did my mother try to smack me. I must have been very naughty to tempt her. I can still see myself dancing around her in the kitchen with her holding on to me with one hand and swinging a wooden spoon in the other. I kept crying: 'Mummy, don't! Mummy don't!' covering my behind with one hand. In the end she gave up, and I got away with a severe warning.

I was not allowed to be too fussy with the food my mother put in front of me. I had to eat it, or I went without that day and had it put in front of me again the following day. The only thing I hated was spinach. It looked so horrible, but eventually I had to finish it the next day, poking my fork around the plate and looking at my mother hoping she would let me off; but she was adamant.

Every morning, without grumbling, Richard and I swallowed a teaspoon of cod liver oil to prevent rickets. I loved it, whereas most children hated the taste.

As my father came from a fairly large family – three brothers, one sister and also a half-brother – and my mother had one sister, Richard and I had quite a few aunts and uncles and various cousins. Unfortunately, my grandfather on my father's side died about five months after I was born, and my grandmother on my mother's side died even earlier.

I loved visiting Aunt Anita and my two cousins Lotte and Erika, who lived in a huge flat within walking distance. My cousins had a playroom each, filled with toys. I enjoyed riding down their broad, long hall on a tricycle. In front of the block was a park with a large rectangular paddling pool surrounded by a broad low brick wall. Richard, on one occasion, climbed up onto the brick wall and toddled along until he fell in. I have never seen my cousin Lotte run so fast (she was 12 years older than me). She jumped in after him, held on to him by the collar of his jacket like a dog, and pulled him out, dripping wet. He screamed his head off and wriggled like mad, trying to get away; but she held on to him and carried him back to the flat, where my mother took over, taking off his wet clothes and drying him.

I have to thank Aunt Anita for giving me her *Ahnenpass* (record book of ancestors) in the seventies. From that, I was able to trace my ancestors back to the middle of the eighteenth century on my mother's side. I heard about these books after the war, But had never seen one. Those belonging to my parents must have been lost during the bombing of our flat, but my aunt had hers with her when she got bombed out. Every adult had to obtain one when Hitler was in power, to prove they were not Jewish.

My parents never talked about such things, even after the war when the dreadful atrocities came to light. Richard and I were still too young then to understand it. One thing is sure, that they cannot have agreed with many aspects of the Third Reich. All political parties, except the Nazi party, were banned in 1933. My father belonged to the *Stahlhelm* (steel helmet), One of the offshoots of those abolished parties. He resigned forcefully, threw his membership card on the table and walked out. When I was older, he told me that he was very angry and disappointed, wondering why all those parties did not unite to stand up against Hitler. No wonder I never saw a picture of Hitler in our flat.

2

Standing on the platform in the cool hall under the glass-domed roof of the main station in Hamburg, I did not realise then I was leaving my sheltered life in our flat for ever.

The train arrived at last. My mother gave me a big bag of sweets, more than I had had after my first day at school. It cheered me up a bit. We all had little satchels and a name-tag on a piece of string hanging around our neck. I shared a compartment on the train with five other children, all looking at the bags of sweets on our laps. When we suddenly noticed the train was starting to move, we dashed to the windows to wave goodbye to our families, scattering the sweets as we did so. I left the train at Graal-Müritz, the Baltic Sea spa near Rostock, with many other children. I remember a great house with gardens. The dining room was as big as a hall, with long wooden tables and benches. There were many toys and books, which I loved, although I could not read properly yet.

Even there life was not safe, and we had to get up once during the night and seek a flak shelter. From there we watched colourful lights, which were called Christmas trees, being dropped by Pathfinders, and heard rumbling noises.

I often wondered why nobody collected me. Most of the children left after three or four weeks, and I should have gone home after a month, but I was still there afterwards. The home was quieter now.

There must have been about 30 children left, and we were split up into smaller bedrooms which slept four.

15

One afternoon during our nap after lunch a nurse woke me up and said my father was downstairs to collect me. What joy! My father had come to take me home. I could not get downstairs fast enough, not realising what a state I was in. My father nearly did not recognise me. I was covered from head to toe in scabies. To this day I still carry the scars. He nearly went mad, accusing the staff of neglect – this was not surprising, considering what my father had been through, as I found out afterwards.

He had come home on special leave towards the end of July 1943, when word went round that Hamburg had been experiencing the most horrific bombing of the war so far. All he found left in our road were heaps of rubble and an axe without its shaft where our block of flats used to be. Where were my mother and my brother Richard? They had had to rush out of the underground shelter when the water pipes burst during the bombing and the air was getting thinner all the time and very smoky.

To me it is still a miracle how they could have survived. They dipped blankets into the water, wrapped them around their bodies and found their way somehow to a tall bunker in Hasselbrook. The bunker had been hit by bombs several times, but withstood the attacks with its thick concrete walls. Sheer instinct for survival must have set in. I dread to think what must have gone through my mother's mind seeing the devastation and the suffering.

My mother's sister, Aunt Anita, said to me in 1970 when I told her I intended to marry an Englishman: 'Your mother would turn in her grave if she knew about this.' Somehow I doubt it. We were the next generation, and most ordinary people detest wars with the horrendous sufferings involved. My mother was a most kind and intelligent woman, liberal and free-thinking, having grown up and lived and worked in Hamburg, a city which was called, not without reason, 'the Gate to the World'. She must have realised that Hitler had to be stopped somehow in his megalomania. However, she might not have agreed with the way the bombing was carried out, trying to wipe out purely civilian areas in

16

Hamburg, especially when the industry was kept well apart from the residential areas; but that was one price to pay for starting a war.

A few days after the disaster, registration points were set up in Hamburg, and my father found to his great joy that my mother and brother had survived and were evacuated to a place near the Danish border. He had to walk out of Hamburg. There was no transport available until he reached a railway station in the north of the city. After he found them both well, staying at a farmhouse in a small village, he had to find his way to Graal-Müritz to collect me.

In the meantime railway tracks were being repaired again somehow, and we could travel into Hamburg to change trains to meet up with my mother and brother at the farmhouse. I still could not believe that we had lost everything, and asked my father if we had time to see our street once more. What I saw was unbelievable. At the end of Rossberg, a brick wall blocked our way, and two wardens guarded it: they said there was danger of epidemics, like typhoid, as many people were buried there. When my father explained that we had lived there, they let us through, warning us to be careful. I could not recognise anything. Where was our block of flats? Where was the dairy? Where was the corner shop? And my school! What had happened to it? Where was the road? And the trees? And where was the archway? All were gone! There were just heaps of rubble, but my father knew somehow where we used to live and pointed to where he had found the axe head. I cried about my lost dolls.

When we arrived at the farm, we were overjoyed at being together again. My mother had a hereditary faulty heart valve and she did not feel too good after the horrifying last few weeks. The farmer thought he had an extra hand in my mother, with most of the men fighting in the war, but she was really not capable of hard physical work for long hours on a farm. Without hesitation my father decided to take us away to Austria. One of his comrades had offered to put us up in his house if the worse came to the worst and we lost our home. So my father re-applied for more leave to take us to a small village called Neumarkt, in Pongau, the alpine area around Salzburg.

I remember a train journey, which never seemed to end. The trains were overcrowded, and I was lifted through a window by my father and put in the string luggage rack above the seats. He shouted to some very merry officers in this compartment for being so ignorant and not knowing what was going on around them, and asked them to make room for us, which they did. My brother slept in the opposite luggage rack. When the train came to a halt at one station, everybody had to get off. We waited the whole night on a platform. Fortunately, the September nights were still warm, and Richard and I just curled up on a blanket under the bench my parents were sitting on, and went to sleep. We were woken up to squeeze onto yet another train. It was sheer pandemonium. There were thousands of people, screaming children and soldiers everywhere; but my brother and I found it very exciting. It was like going on a big adventure. I was sad at having lost all my toys, especially my dolls, but I was happy having my father there for so long, not realising that it was only days before he had to go back to war again.

Eventually we reached Neumarkt and jumped down onto the just slightly raised hard ground which was the platform.

At the gate, we were met by Mrs Lehrl and her daughter Anni, who was about ten years old. This was the family we were going to stay with. Richard and I walked along with Anni, while my parents talked to Mrs Lehrl. We could hardly understand what Anni was saying, as she spoke a completely different dialect to us. It was a very long walk along the road to the village, but we did not have much to carry. Everything looked completely different. There were no blocks of flats, just single houses now and then along the road, and wide open fields. When we came closer to the village, the number of single-storey houses increased along the slightly upward-sloping road.

I did not realise until quite a few years later that the following two years would be the happiest of my entire childhood.

3

We stopped in front of a very big house situated along the main road. It was a guest house, and looked enormous to me, coming from a one-bedroom flat. At the back were trees and shrubs, flowers and a sloping path which led to gardens and some detached houses. There were so many rooms. I had to sleep in the lounge on the settee with the grandfather clock behind my head. It made me jump when I heard it chiming for the first time. It disturbed my nights to start with, but then I became used to it and slept through. From the lounge, a door led to the bedroom in which my mother and Richard slept. My father could not stay, he had to leave us again to go back to war. There were more people living upstairs, including a small boy called Dietmar and his mother. They had a small photo studio in one of the rooms. My mother took us once to have our photo taken. It is the only one I have of her with us children.

Soon I had to go to school. I did not like it very much. Being a Protestant in a Catholic village and an outsider with a different dialect made it very difficult settling in. I was called horrible names. The worst one was *Preussisches Bombenpack* (Prussian bomb crowd). It really upset me, especially as I came from Hamburg, not Prussia.

However, soon we were picking up the local dialect and many new, different words, so that my mother had problems at times understanding us. Mrs Lehrl took in another family with two children who lived downstairs in an annex. There was also a large wooden storeroom in which all the children played. We had great times there on rainy days. At last I had some friends to play with.

By December, there was snow everywhere. None of the children I knew had sledges, so we borrowed the biggest cast-iron frying pan I had ever seen in my life. Richard and I could comfortably sit in it. He sat in front of me, and we both bent over to hold on to the long wooden handle for dear life, spinning round and round and sliding down the icy slope, where we fell in a heap. Many children had short skis and started skiing as soon as they could walk. Sometimes they let me borrow a pair; but I never quite got the hang of it and fell spreadeagled halfway down the slope in a pile of snow.

Christmas arrived. We decorated a small Christmas tree in the hall with little red apples and small bits of cotton wool. There was a lot of baking going on, and the smell wafted through the whole house out into the garden. All the children took it in turns to lick the bowl until there was not a single scrap left. We watched each other like hawks to make sure nobody took an extra turn. We also had the slightly burned biscuits as samples. On Christmas Eve we had our presents, which were hand-knitted jumpers and mittens. There was no money for toys, but we did not miss them. We always played out in the snow or made up games in our storeroom.

There was still snow, slowly melting, on the ground the following Easter. Early in the morning on Easter Sunday, Anni, Richard and I went to the meadows around the nearby Waller Lake, each carrying a small basket to pick snowflakes, which look slightly larger than snowdrops. I have never again in my life seen so many snowflakes. It was unbelievable, they were everywhere. Anni showed us exactly how to pick them without pulling out the roots. At an early age we were learning about conservation. When we came back, we gave the baskets, which were overflowing with beautiful snowflakes, to our mothers and went Easter-egg hunting in the garden. Eventually we found them, hidden in a hollow of the wooden shed, lying in a nest lined with moss: six colourful boiled eggs, two for each of us. Our mothers must have been busy while we were out.

Shortly afterwards we moved to the house next door. The lady there, whom we called Tante Höller, offered my mother and us a room on the first floor of her home. She had seen how exhausted my mother was, working too hard all the time in Mrs Lehrl's house. Tante Höller was a kind woman who must have been in her fifties. She always wore dark skirts and blouses and an apron which covered most of her skirt. There was a small hardware shop downstairs. Opposite it, through a large wooden door, we entered the huge square kitchen with an enormous range on one side. It was much larger than the one we used to have in our flat in Hamburg. In the middle of the kitchen stood a big wooden table surrounded by chairs.

It was lovely having a big room all to ourselves upstairs, and I was happy that we three could all sleep in the double bed. No more grandfather clock! At the end of the bed stood a small table and three chairs, where we had our meals. In one corner there was a green-tiled tall stove which nearly reached the ceiling. We always had a kettle boiling in the small niche in the middle of it which was shut by two little wrought iron doors. We also had baked apples in it, which smelt delicious. It did not smell so delicious when I hid a small metal bowl there with a concoction of spices, including salt, pepper, paprika, cloves and sugar – more or less everything I could lay my hands on from our dresser – when I heard my mother coming up the stairs. That was my first try at cooking.

On the same floor lived Oma (Grandmother) Dachgruber, who was in her eighties. I liked her very much. I often went to see her. She read me stories from a small book and listened to my little worries. In return, I would get some food from her larder or fetch the butter for her from the cool cellar, where small red apples were stored on the wooden shelves. Tante Höller must have wondered why the supply slowly went down. Richard and I were always hungry. With most food being rationed, there was just never enough to feed us growing children.

My brother's dream was having a whole loaf scooped out

and filled with sugar. His wish was granted when he took a small white loaf from our breadbin one afternoon, hollowed it out and filled it with the remaining sugar we had. That was to be his picnic when he disappeared, taking the cart with him. I did not think much of it until he did not turn up when it was teatime. I became worried then and told my mother what had happened. Everybody started searching. A dozen or so adults looked for him all over the whole village and then began combing the surrounding areas. Just before sunset he was found eventually near a farm, fast asleep under a tree. When he came back he was asleep again; but this time curled up and wrapped in a blanket, lying in the cart, which was pulled by his rescuer, a farmer. My mother was so relieved she bundled him straight off to bed. That was the first time one of us went to bed unwashed and dirty.

We envied Dietmar from next door, whose mother often sent him out with a slice of buttered bread which had sugar sprinkled on top. How we tried to persuade him to let us have a bite, but to no avail.

On the opposite side of the road and further along, we could see the school and the church with its prominent tower, which always had a power of attraction to Richard and me. I liked to look quietly around the cool church, while my brother preferred the bell tower. There was no vandalism then, and all the doors were unlocked. I opened one heavy side door once, then stepped back a pace quickly. In this small whitewashed room a dead woman was laid out. She looked peaceful and regal, but the coolness of the room hit me and made me shiver. This was my first meeting with death.

Suddenly I heard the sound of the church bell. I thought it was strange. There was no service or funeral. My brother came into mind. Where was he? I charged around to the bell tower, and there he was, nearly lifted off the ground by the rope. I tore him away and we dashed home. What if the fire brigade came out? But nothing happened, and nobody ever found out. We only told my mother, and I was not sure how she would react to it. But she had a sense of humour and did not tell him off.

23

The summer holidays were very hot and never-ending. In August we all went to help a farmer in the next village with the haymaking. My brother's and my shoes were by now much too small, and we went around barefoot like most of the village children. We did not mind the stubble fields, having grown thick skin on the soles of our feet, and we walked down to the lake to the open-air swimming pool to splash about in the cool water.

My mother and all the other women who had found new homes with their children in our village and surrounding areas went on courses to freshen up their knowledge of shorthand, typewriting and other office tasks. My mother also spoke English, which was going to be a great asset the following year. Before her marriage to my father in September 1934 she had worked for an import and export company, which was probably trading with Great Britain, as many companies were in Hamburg.

So we were more or less left to our own devices with not much supervision, but we were safe. There was a sawmill in our village, another splendid but dangerous playground, and we were never allowed to go there unless Anni came with us. I can still smell the sawdust, which was piled up high in the mill. The high stacks of pine planks were ideal for playing hide-and-seek between, and we waded to the river along the narrow open pipes into which the huge waterwheel sent cascades of water. Anni, being a very good swimmer, took my brother across the river on her back. I was so worried in case he slipped off and drowned, and shouted at her all the time to come back. But my brother was quite safe with her and enjoyed it tremendously.

When we heard there was buttermilk available at one of the dairies well outside the village, we walked a long distance to buy some for my mother. We were lucky when we were offered a lift back by a farmer on his waggon drawn by two oxen, but by the time we came home our metal jug was half empty. Buttermilk was cool and refreshing on a hot summer's day. When we had milk which was slightly off, we kept it in a bowl for a day. By then it had set in the hot

24

weather and we ate it with sugar. It was called *Dick-Milch* (thick milk).

We roamed the countryside in a group of four to five children. It was safe, and my mother was not particularly worried about letting us loose. Often we came home with grass-stained clothes when we rolled down the green hills. Our mother was not very amused by that. Now and then from somewhere a chicken appeared on the menu. Once we saw one when it was still alive, running about in the yard behind the house. One of the young men who worked for Tante Höller in the workshop caught it and chopped its head off on the block. We screamed when it dropped to the ground and still moved about without the head. We were children from a city and not yet toughened up by country life. Another episode filled us with disgust, when we watched children wading in a brook outside the village, catching frogs by the dozens, pulling their legs off, and throwing the legless bodies back into the brook. I still would not eat frog's legs even if I were paid for it. There are limits.

A four-year-old boy who came along on one of our explorations complained that something was crawling about in his short trousers and began to cry. Being the eldest in our little group, just eight years old, I had the job of investigating. So I pulled his trousers and pants down, to see a long wriggly tapeworm. I picked a couple of leaves as I did not feel like touching this horrible worm, and pulled it slowly out of his bottom. I dropped it in disgust. The little boy was so relieved. When we told his mother about it afterwards, she asked me if I had noticed the head coming out as well, otherwise it would keep on growing. I was not too sure about that.

One evening during the summer of 1944 I heard voices in the big kitchen, one of them my mother's. I heard snippets of 'Putsch went wrong. Poor Stauffenberg! Hitler got away!' When I opened the door, it went quiet, then my mother and Tante Höller began talking about the dinner.

In the autumn it was back to school. But instead of

coming home afterwards, we went to a kindergarten, with other children whose mothers had to work now, as the menfolk were on the front line. My mother worked in the large *Amtszimmer* (office) of the mayor of Neumarkt, where ration cards, birth and death certificates etc. were given out. We did our homework in the kindergarten and played. We were also taught to sing propaganda songs about the Hitler Youth movement. One particular song I can still remember to this day. My mother did not like it at all, especially when she was being pressed into giving her consent for Richard to join the Hitler Youth movement. She flatly refused and took us out of the kindergarten. After all, he was only six years old then. She did not like our minds being poisoned at such a tender age. After that, we stayed at home after school or played in the yard. Tante Höller was always around. Quite often we turned up at the mayor's office to see our mother. There were always people queuing in front of the glass-partitioned counter.

One Sunday in the autumn, Tante Höller took us three with her into the woods. We pulled along behind us a fairly large cart containing empty sacks. It was great fun spending most of the day in the woods collecting cones and filling the sacks with them. They were to be our winter fuel. We paused near a sparkling brook to have our *Jause* (lunch), consisting of a slab of rye bread, goat's-milk cheese and refreshing cool water from the brook. When the sun went lower, all the sacks were loaded onto the cart, and we pulled it along to a farm where Tante Höller had asked for it to be stored until somebody could deliver it to the house.

One day we all went by train to Salzburg. Near the station was a bridge spanning the river Salzach. We walked along the Getreidegasse with its high buildings and wrought-iron shop signs depicting the various wares. Weary and tired, we ended up in one of the cafés.

It was still early afternoon, so we decided to see one of the attractions of Mozart's town, the high fortress Hohensalzburg which towers over the old city. We had a marvellous view from the eleventh-century castle on this clear and sunny day. It had been an exciting outing, and we were absolutely exhausted when we went to bed that evening.

Another excursion I can remember was to Hallstatt, a delightful lakeside place. A beautiful big park with fountains in the shape of animals appears in my mind. I was always fascinated by water, and seeing those huge animals spurting water non-stop from their mouths was a great attraction to me. My mother had to drag me away when it was time to go home.

It must have been November when my mother received a letter from the army. My father was missing, presumed dead. He had been in Russia, withdrawing from the advancing Russian Army. We were very sad. I could not believe that we would never see my father again. But we still had a ray of hope that he would come back.

Shortly afterwards, towards the Christmas of 1944, many hundreds of refugees from Hungary swamped our village, pulling all their belongings in carts. Their clothing was completely different from ours. The women wore colourful skirts, embroidered blouses and waistcoats. The mayor offered them our school to stay in, but hopes of not having to go to school were short-lived. We were taught in the restaurant of an inn, sitting on wooden benches around a tall, tiled wood-burning stove.

It was very exciting coming up to Christmas. My mother and many other women were very busy making life a little bit more comfortable for the poor people. We spent every spare minute at the school, helping to make it more festive for Christmas. One farmer brought a huge Christmas tree into the hall, and everybody contributed different decorations. Even candles appeared from somewhere. We laid the long tables for Christmas Eve and decorated them with little Christmas tree branches along the middle. I do not know where all the food came from, but most people kept chickens and contributed some of them. During all these festive activities we joined in with the Christmas carol-singing, and somebody played an accordion. My mother,

Richard and I spent most of Christmas Eve at the school, being refugees ourselves in a way. Everybody was so friendly to us, and I received presents from a couple of ladies. One was a rag doll, which I kept until well into my teenage years. The other present was most welcome in the freezing winter as I always suffered from cold feet; it was a beautifully embroidered pair of black bedsocks.

When we came back, Tante Höller lit the few candles we had on the Christmas tree in the big kitchen. She was on her own. Her husband and two sons were away fighting in the war. We sat around the table, drinking *Ersatzkaffee* (an artificial 'coffee' made from roasted corn) and eating home-made cakes and biscuits. We sang more Christmas carols, with my mother's beautiful soprano voice surpassing ours. The range and the candles sent a warm glow through the darkened kitchen, and now and then the burning pine cones exploded with a pop in the range.

The new year 1945 brought many excitements into our lives. Soon the Hungarian refugees left, and we went back into our school building.

My mother still tried hard to feed us ever-hungry children. Once she took me with her to the bakery, hoping to barter some of the tobacco ration stamps for a loaf. The baker showed us around and then took a tray of loaves out of the oven. The smell was delicious, but I touched the hot tray with my fingers. Without thinking, I raced home as if stung by a tarantula, and up the stairs to fill our washing bowl with cool water from the tap on our landing. I was still immersing my burning hands when my mother came home, wondering what happened to me, carrying a loaf in her hand. I never had any blisters or burns. I must have done this instinctively as the usual remedy for burns in those days was the application of butter or flour. Only a few years ago it was scientifically proved that iced water avoids blisters after burns.

We had snow well into early spring. Now and then four oxen pulled a wooden snowplough along the village road, piling more snow at its edges. We loved jumping into it from

28

the high stone wall in front of the house, getting soaked in the process.

We had one rug in our room, which my mother took outside from time to time to give it a good beating with a carpet beater; but during the winter she laid it on the clean snow in the back of the house and used the carpet beater on it. The rug always came up as new, and the snow became dirty.

The sun's rays got warmer, and from underneath the eaves huge icicles kept dripping. The icy drops burst on impact and spattered our shoes. My mother kept calling: 'Don't go too close to the icicles, in case they come crashing down!' With a low thud the sheets of snow from the sloping roofs exploded onto the gravel path. Spring was certainly on its way and with it large fields of snowflakes along the Waller Lake. Cowslips blossomed along the paths, and the house martins were back under the eaves busy repairing their nests from the previous year. Soon the tiny heads of baby birds were looking out of the nests and demanding food from their parents. Spring had come.

Life went on. I still did not like school very much, and my brother and I continued to be naughty at times.

My worst subject at school was needlecraft. I struggled with the knitting and kept dropping stitches. I envied the girls who had advanced to cable knitting while I was still struggling to learn the elementary stitches, and became so upset that I decided to play truant. Instead of going to school, I hid on the stairs which led from our floor to the drying loft, not realising that it was Monday, and washday. I must have been sitting there for less than an hour when my mother came up the stairs laden with her washing basket. She nearly dropped it when she saw me sitting there with a guilt-ridden face. Then she took me straight back to school, and I never skipped school again.

I still feel ashamed now about the following story because I caused my mother a lot of unnecessary worry. She cooked a big pot of potato soup one day. We ate half in our room, then stored the other half in the pot in the cool cellar for the

29

next day. Richard and I were asked to bring it upstairs to be heated up. But we could not wait. We ate nearly half of it cold, from the ladle, standing in the cellar. I was worried about what we had done so I topped it up with water from the tap and took it to our room. Then we ran off and hid, my brother in the workroom behind the house, and me in a sand-filled shed next to the house. I heard my mother calling for us, and she eventually found my brother. I can still hear her calling my name now over and over again. It was getting dark, and I came slowly out of my hiding place. My mother was standing in front of the house, worried sick. Tante Höller pulled me into the kitchen and made me kneel down in front of my mother to beg her forgiveness. My brother was already in bed when I crept in. We had no more soup, and hungrily watched my mother eating the thin soup at our little table. The next day, my mother said: 'Fancy hiding in the shed where all the dogs go!' Years later I understood why she was so frantically searching for me.

The Americans had already marched in and taken Austria by spring 1945. For us children it meant chewing gum and chocolate, and new friends. There was one empty room left on our floor, and four American soldiers moved in. Tante Höller must have had her hands full with washing all the bed linen. When Richard and I went to see them to say hello, we were shocked to see two of them lying on the clean bed linen with their boots on. They let us look out of their window with binoculars, and I thought I could touch the school with my hands. By then it was not our school any more. The Americans lived in it, and for us it meant being taught at the inn again.

I still remember the anticipation of everybody when we were told the Americans were coming. We hung a white sheet out of one of the upstairs windows as a sign of capitulation, and we were not allowed to go out. The mayor of Neumarkt drove along the road in his open car shouting through a megaphone: 'Stay indoors!' We also pulled the curtains on a lovely sunny day, but Richard and I peeped out. We heard the rumbling noise of the tanks long before we could see them. And there they were. They just fitted into the deep road between the high stone walls on both sides. There were so many, it went on for ages. Eventually my mother told us to come away from the window, and we had dinner. The next day there were more and more coming, not just tanks, but also jeeps and motorbikes. By then we were not afraid any more, and all the children and some adults lined the street and watched. The Americans won us over very quickly when they threw chocolates and sweets from the tanks. Such rarities! We soon learned some English, like: 'Thank you, do you have any chewing gum or chocolate, please?' I always curtsied, saying: 'Thank you', and my brother always bowed his head. We were well brought up by our parents. It must have seemed strange to the American soldiers, I think.

For some weeks we were not allowed to go into the woods. The Americans were hunting down German SS soldiers who were hiding there.

Next to our house stood a large *Gasthof* (inn) which the Americans also occupied. From the back of our house, my brother and I squeezed along a shed and hopped over a fence, ending up in the backyard of the inn, where the dustbins stood. We always looked carefully around to see if anybody was watching us before we lifted off the lids of the dustbins, looking for anything edible. We could not believe our eyes how much food the soldiers threw out. We always came back home with something like a piece of cake, some bread or half a pancake. But somebody must have seen us, though. When we went again the following day, we found four pancakes wrapped up in newspaper on top of one of the dustbin lids. How marvellous, they must have been put there just for us! The Americans were well known for loving children. We were very happy having this extra food and told our mother about it then.

Spring turned into summer, and we were running about again barefoot. With raw materials for producing hardware for the shop unobtainable, Tante Höller and her two apprentices thought of the great idea of recycling the used tins the Americans left in enormous mountains near the Waller Lake. Pulling an open cart behind us, we all walked down to the lake to sort through them. For the first time in my life I smelt pineapples. Quite often the tins were not completely empty, and Richard and I were absorbed in sniffing the contents, which by then did not look good enough to eat, and trying to read the black print on the tins. It did not take long to fill up the cart, and we walked home excitedly.

We helped wash the tins thoroughly in a trough in the yard. In the process we ended up getting soaked. Keeping a safe distance, we were fascinated watching the two apprentices in their workshop turning the tin cans into various-sized saucepans, colanders and cutlery. It was a long process to see the shiny end product. The tins had to be cut open, flattened and soldered together first of all, then cut and shaped again in one of the many vices. Richard and I were only too happy taking the small open cart down to the lake to collect more supplies for the workshop. It was great fun sitting in the cart behind each other, with my brother holding the *Deichsel* (the handle used to pull and steer the cart) to keep straight on the sloping path down to the lake. Soon the shop had many more customers. Even the Americans came now and then to have a look around and buy some items. My mother seemed to be the only person who could speak English, and she helped out in the shop when she had time.

By then we had some good American friends, especially from the inn next door. We saw them nearly every day, and sometimes one of them visited us in the kitchen downstairs to bring us a tall tin of pancake batter or a handful of bones, sometimes with meat, with which to make some stock. The pancakes were always a feast. One day after school Richard and I each had our first orange from an officer. We were speechless. What beautiful colour! And the smell! We turned them over and over again before we ate them. They tasted sweet and juicy.

In our spare time after school we were often found

hanging about in the big gateway leading to the courtyard of another inn further along on the other side of the road, watching the soldiers washing the piles of dishes in very long wooden troughs, made from hollowed-out tree-trunks, in the cool shady gateway. One of them cut himself badly on his wrist with a knife in the washing-up water. The blood dripped to the floor, and somebody bandaged his arm with a piece of cloth. They asked us where the nearest doctor was and then drove in their jeep at high speed along the village path to the surgery near the church. Later in the afternoon we went back to find out how he was. He was sitting in a chair in the shade with the wrist bandaged and his arm in a sling. He smiled at us, and when we came closer to have a better look, he said, 'Thank you' and gave us both a small bar of chocolate. By the time we marched home we had eaten the chocolate. My mother asked us if we had a piece left for her, and I felt quite guilty about having been so greedy and not thinking of her.

Most of the soldiers smoked, and threw their cigarette ends carelessly away. All the children, including us, collected the stubs. Richard and I had a little metal box in which we used to put them. When we could not cram any more into it, we peeled the paper off and gave the tobacco to our mother, who exchanged it for a little bit of extra food.

We were always trying to supplement our meals. The meadows were beautiful and full of sweet smells during the summer months. They contained many different plants and flowers and our mother would ask Richard and me to pick young leaves of sorrel and nettles. They were ideal as a substitute for spinach – not one of our favourite meals. When we were given some fresh eggs, my mother preserved them in a large glass jar. We had never heard of refrigerators then. Along the woodland path behind the school we found wild strawberries and raspberries, and we picked fragrant woodruff for Tante Höller, who used it for making punch with home-made wine and lemonade. It was always pleasantly cool under the trees on a hot day.

33

* * *

Richard and I did not realise that the war had been over since May when our mother told us in late summer that we had the choice either to stay in Neumarkt or go back to Hamburg. She decided to go back with us, even though she had a job at the mayor's office and we were happy in Neumarkt. I liked Tante Höller and Oma Dachgruber very much and could not bear not seeing them again, and we had many friends among the Americans as well. But we also wanted to know what had happened to our relatives in Hamburg, and, who knows, perhaps our father would come back to Hamburg from Russia.

My mother had a lot to organise. In those two years we had accumulated some personal belongings again, which had to be packed. The two apprentices at the workshop built a solid wooden box, which was about 125 centimetres square and 75 centimetres high, a size which was going to cause us quite a few problems on our long journey back to Hamburg. Oma Dachgruber gave me the small Austrian story book from which she used to read to me, and a delicate little vase with flower patterns. To this day I still treasure these two presents. The vase, made in 1873, is antique now. It survived many moves, and I love to use it for the first small spring flowers from our garden.

It was the autumn of 1946 when we eventually left for Passau, on the German border. This was the destination the coach driver had been paid to take us and many other women and children to. But every time we stopped along the way, he refused to go any further. It was a nightmare. The smaller children cried, and the women shouted and pleaded and begged the driver to take us to Passau. My mother and the other women had to give him money, food and tobacco. He certainly was taking advantage of our situation. Eventually we arrived there late in the evening, totally exhausted.

We spent the night in a waiting room at the railway station, sitting, then sleeping, on our big box. My mother

34

always relied on some kind person to lift it onto a luggage trolley at our various stops.

We travelled in an open goods waggon at one time. It was pouring with rain, and we became soaking wet. Then we stopped along the line, level with another train. Many tired-looking men, perhaps prisoners of war or foreign workers, looked out at us and my kind mother gave them a box of cigars to share between them, and they gave us some sweets. She always saved the tobacco stamps she needed in exchange for cigars or cigarettes for my father, just in case he came back.

We started moving again, and passed a large railway station, which we saw was Bremen, where we needed to change trains. The station disappeared behind us, and we were still moving along, but at a slower pace now. My mother was worried and jumped from the waggon, running alongside the goods train to try to reach the driver, all the time shouting, 'Halt! Halt!' Richard and I were calling after her to come back. We were worried in case the train drove on and left my mother behind. Eventually the driver must have spotted my mother, and stopped in a goods siding. Now we had the problem of getting back to the station. But help was at hand. Some kind men helped my mother with the huge box. A single steam locomotive was going back to the station platform to take a train to Hamburg. The only way of getting the box onto the locomotive was by squeezing it between the railings and steps which led to the driver's seat. It took three men to heave and push the heavy box into place and secure it with rope. We squeezed in from the other side, standing next to the driver, with my mother standing on the steps and holding onto the railings.

Soon we were back on one of the platforms in Bremen. The box came down again and ended up in a goods carriage on our train to Hamburg. The sun came out and made the raindrops glisten on the platform, and the locomotive whistled and pushed out big white clouds of steam. We went into the next carriage behind our box and found some empty wooden seats. Many different questions went

35

through my mind. What would Hamburg be looking like? Where were we going to stay? The latter question was soon answered by my mother; we were going to stay with Aunt Anita and our cousins Erika and Charlotte.

It was a long journey. The train stopped at several stations and along the track. Along the way I saw many bombed-out areas, bare high brick walls and a couple of tall chimneys reaching to the sky. At last in the distance the *Elb-Brücken* (three bridges crossing the river Elbe) appeared in the mist. The train rattled over the railway sleepers while crossing the river, and soon we reached the main station in Hamburg. But what a sight! There were hardly any windows left in the huge dome-shaped roof; the metal frames were twisted, and we could see the dark sky through them. And, as on the way out of Hamburg two years before, there were people and soldiers – this time English ones, in their brown uniforms – everywhere. The noise and the crowds were bewildering. My mother had to arrange for the box to be delivered to our new address, and then we squeezed our way out of the station, anxiously hanging on to her.

4

Aunt Anita lived in one room on the first floor of a block of flats in the Kaiser-Wilhelm-Strasse, near the city centre. Downstairs used to be a wicker-furniture shop, where my grandfather worked until the bombing; but now it was mostly devastated. So was half of the house at one side. We occupied the room next to my aunt's. There was also my cousin Erika, who was about 13 years old. My older cousin Lotte was still in the Land Army, staying on for an extra year. My grandfather lived in a part of the attic which was still habitable. To the delight of my brother and myself, half of the brick wall between the two rooms was missing, and we had some fantastic pillow fights with Erika across the wall in the evenings. The broad staircase to the third floor, which led to a row of communal toilets, was still intact, with its linoleum and part of the wooden bannister. There was no electric light up there. Opposite the toilets the wall had disappeared and some of the toilet doors were missing. We could see the outside and the stars above in the evenings when my mother took us there before bedtime. It was too dangerous to go on our own in the evenings, just in case we went too close to the edge. Our box, which had arrived in the meantime, served us as a table. Apart from single bunk beds, we had no furniture, but it did not matter.

There was no school to go to for the time being. Many schools were bombed out, and teachers had to be found or recruited back from retirement.

My brother and I spent most of our time outside, playing in the heaps of rubble that we saw everywhere. Rubble women in aprons and headscarfs were everywhere, sorting out bricks and knocking off the mortar with trowels so they could be used again.

We had ration cards, and both of us went regularly to a baker's shop to buy maize bread, which was very heavy and solid. There was one very narrow road left nearby with cobblestones and terraced houses, Bäckerbreitergang (baker's broad walk), which mostly escaped the bombing. The only other similar small road of this kind still existing is called the Kramer Amts Buildings, opposite the St Michaelis Church, which were built in 1670 by the Mercers' Guild for the widows of guild members. This is now a very popular tourist attraction, being one of the few relics of old Hamburg left. St Michaelis Church, the emblem of Hamburg – called *Unser Michel* (our Michael) by the local inhabitants – is another tourist attraction. It was rebuilt in almost its old baroque style after a fire destroyed it in 1906, and again after extensive damage during the Second World War. The 132-metre-high copper-domed tower, the highest and most impressive of the five church towers in the city, greets everybody who comes down the river Elbe. From the platform of the clock tower, which is 106 metres above sea level, one can only marvel at the magnificent view of the city and the busy harbour. The former surroundings have completely changed. Now it stands as an imposing monument representing the Protestant church, isolated at the edge of the Ost-West Straße, a broad through-road.

Aunt Anita told us some stories of how she and her younger daughter Erika, who had a heart problem, survived; but the most wonderful one she told us was that many people in Hamburg believed that there was a future again after the terrible bombings when they noticed that many charred horse chestnut and lilac trees were in blossom again in the autumn of 1945. It really cheered her up after losing everything, even though the seasons for those trees were completely mixed up.

One Sunday in November my Aunt Else, my father's only sister, invited us for coffee and cake in the afternoon. She lived in Horn, another area of Hamburg, in a one-bedroom flat with my uncle Willi and cousin Karl-Heinz, after being bombed out in Wandsbek. She had invited about ten of our relatives, who were all sitting around the festive table in the lounge when we arrived after a journey by tram from the city. I wondered why there were so many of our relatives there. It was nobody's birthday. We said 'Hello' to everybody, then my aunt said there was another visitor in the bedroom through the adjoining door. Richard and I went through first, with my mother behind us. I could not believe my eyes when I saw my father sitting at the window eating raw onions. I kept calling out excitedly over and over again: 'Our daddy is back again, our daddy is back again!' My mother just hugged him and sobbed, 'Otto! Otto!' Now we were a proper family once more.

But my father was so thin! He had just stubble on his head as the Russians had shaved every prisoner of war for hygienic reasons. Lice were very common in prisoner-of-war camps. He was sent home from Siberia because he was too thin and too weak to work, he said. He only weighed 38 kilos. They gave him his papers and put him with other prisoners on a train going west. When the train stopped he and other soldiers just had to keep on walking. Crossing the border into Germany was the biggest hurdle. He tried to cross it one night with another soldier, who tripped over one of the wires which led from one dugout border post to another. The bells rang in the dugouts, and my father kept saying to him: 'Keep down!' But he stood up, standing out against the searchlights that had suddenly appeared, and got shot. How dreadful to survive a long war and prison camps and then being killed just before reaching home. My father crept back into a nearby wood, where he hid the whole day. The following evening he tried his luck again, and got through.

He told us that he was captured during the retreat of the German Army, feeding the horses for the last time before he had to leave them behind. Thousands of German soldiers were captured by the advancing Russians. The boots were taken off him, and he had to wrap his feet in rags against the freezing cold weather. Then the endless trek to Siberia began. Many prisoners of war died on the way. Once in the camp, they slept on wooden bunks. They had one hunk of bread and some watery soup daily. The Russians themselves had not enough to eat. My father had to dig latrines, not easy in sub-zero temperatures. Typhoid and dysentery were killing many prisoners, and my father kept telling them, to no avail, not to drink the dirty water to quench their terrible thirst. Everybody hid their bread under their straw pillows. When somebody died, fights broke out over the bread. It is really surprising that he survived such an ordeal, but he was very tough and healthy.

My father found us some better accommodation the following week. It was a room in a first-floor flat. Families who had not lost their flats had to take in homeless people by law.

Christmas was upon us. We had no tree or presents, but we were very happy being together again. I slept with my mother in the top bunk, and my father in the bottom one. My brother Richard had a single bunk bed under the window. I started wetting the bed, not a very nice thing to admit; but those unsettling times must have affected me more than I realised. My parents were not very happy about it, but my mother was never cross with me. The mattresses were only thin, and my poor father was woken up by the trickle. I also had lice, and nothing seemed to work getting rid of them, whatever my mother tried. I hated my hair being rinsed with vinegar. It burned my already sore scalp.

For heating we had a little wrought-iron stove, nicknamed *Hexe* because it was completely black and looked like a witch. It burned anything from potato peelings to the wood which my brother and I collected from the rubble of what had been four-storey houses. We never had any rubbish to throw out. Our landlady's grown-up son slept in the adjacent room. He always came home late in the evenings, when we were already in bed, waking us up as he came through our room. He also collected wood each morning from the store on the balcony, which he could only reach from our room. It always seemed to be just when we were getting up. There was not much privacy. We had the stove burning all day, on which was just enough space for one big pot. My mother cooked our meals in it, which mostly consisted of soups and cabbage or swede stew with a few potatoes and, if we were lucky, a tiny piece of pork belly or bones. In the evenings, during the frequent power cuts, we opened the stove door very carefully just a fraction so that we could see what we were eating.

In the new year we started going to school again. I went to a school in the Seilerstrasse, a very old and austere-looking building. My father had his old job back at the Meteorological Office in the Bernhard Nocht Strasse above the harbour, which pleased him very much. The office had been moved there from the previous site nearby at the *Stintfang* (smelt catch), high above the harbour. The bombed-out building had not been completely devastated, and we understood why it had been called the *Umgestülpte Kommode* (upside-down chest of drawers). Eventually it was pulled down and replaced with a very popular youth hostel, from which one has a fantastic view onto the busy harbour down below.

My mother spent most of her time indoors, not feeling too well. There was a lot of snow that winter, and our little stove needed plenty of wood. Richard and I spent every afternoon after school in the rubble collecting wood. There was an enormous wooden beam sticking out of the rubble which we just could not shift. Perhaps our father could come back after work and bring his padsaw. We were very frightened when an old man called over to us, expecting him to tell us off; but he asked us into the little wooden hut he had built right at the back between the rubble. There were stacks of wood piled up neatly outside his hut, and he told us we could take as much as we were able to carry, and to come back with our father in the evening to collect some more.

Richard and I wore hard black ankle boots which were getting too small. As shoes were unobtainable, my father just cut the front of our boots out so our toes could wriggle again, but naturally our woolly socks and feet got wet and frozen stiff. As soon as we got home from our schools we stripped the boots and socks off and dried them near the little stove and warmed our cold feet. Then we were off again to find more firewood.

The forbidden black market was in full swing. People were swopping things for food or buying it at outrageous prices. There are always those who take advantage of the less fortunate. Quite often there were police raids. Everybody tried to run away or hide in the houses; but people who were caught were taken away in the *Grüne Minna* (green police van). There were people trading even in the entrances of our blocks of flats. My parents were worried it would not be safe for us children any more. But Richard and I found it quite exciting, becoming more and more streetwise. We knew exactly which shops had a delivery of food. Regardless of what it was, be it dried potato in the shape of long matchsticks, dried egg powder from the grocers or still hot stock for soups from the butcher, we queued for our mother. But very often we came home with empty hands and very disappointed when the shops ran out before it was our turn.

My poor mother became very ill by the middle of January 1946, and had to go into hospital in Langenhorn in the north of Hamburg, a long way from where we were living. Richard was being looked after by my grandfather and his by now third wife, back at the Kaiser-Wilhelm-Strasse. I had to live with Aunt Else in Horn. My father stayed on in our bedsit on his own. Suddenly we were all split up, having just got used to being a family again. It meant yet another school for me. Beim Pachthof, the road in which the school was situated, was only a five-minute walk away. The teachers there were very friendly, and the girls in my class nice, but I did not have any particular friends. I wondered how long I was going to stay there.

Typhoid had broken out in Hamburg, and everybody had to be vaccinated. Women and girls of all ages queued after school in our school hall to wait for their turn. I found it painful being vaccinated in the breast. We needed three vaccinations at weekly intervals, and I was glad when it was over. By then it was March. My father came regularly to visit me, always bringing something to eat. He spent half of his monthly wages on a heavy maize loaf on the black market, which he shared out between us all. I wondered when I could come home again. But my father said it might not be for quite a while. A couple of times he picked me up from my aunt's on a Sunday to take me to see my mother at the hospital. It was a very long journey; but I was so pleased to see her during the visiting times. She was lying in bed looking very frail and pale. The discovery of penicillin in 1943 helped many patients, including my mother. Even being very ill she never lost her sense of humour and formed a club with other women on the ward who had to stay in for long periods. It was called: The 'quiet' corner. She wrote poems about life in hospital and organised sing-songs when she felt better, inviting the doctors and nurses along.

My aunt had to take in a woman, Frau Sumpffleet, who slept in the lounge. My aunt, uncle, cousin Karl-Heinz and I had to share their only bedroom. Frau Sumpffleet kept her bread in my aunt's dresser in the small kitchen. I must have looked so skinny and hungry all the time that she took pity on me and sometimes gave me a slice of her rationed bread. Once, I was very naughty and stole a 50-gram meat ration stamp from my aunt's purse. On the way to school I bought 200 grams of liver pâté; it was on special offer so I got four times the weight. I paid with the pocket money my father had given me at his last visit. I ate the whole piece of pâté before I arrived at the school gates. My aunt did not notice until a couple of days later that her precious stamp was missing from her purse. She suspected her son, but I had to own up. Luckily she was not too cross with me.

I now acquired a taste for pâté. My uncle's parents lived in a tiny brick house on their allotment, which they had built from rubble. It had a little wooden conservatory where they stored all their bottled fruit, bottled meat from their rabbits

43

and also rabbit pâté. We visited them sometimes on a Sunday afternoon for coffee and home-made cakes. While the adults were busy talking, my cousin and I sneaked into the conservatory and finished nearly a whole jar of their rabbit pâté. We just could not stop eating. Oh, I felt so guilty afterwards. I had a good telling-off the next time we visited them. But my stomach never rebelled; it must have been lined with bricks.

The Easter holidays came and went, and I was back at school, having moved on to the fifth class. One of my aunt's neighbours on the same floor came to see us one afternoon. We were sitting around the little square table in the kitchen when she whispered something to my aunt, who got up and came back with a hand towel and a hairbrush. They told me they had to brush my hair there and then, and spread the hand towel out on the table and started brushing my hair. My head was alive with lice! I lost count how many we squashed with our fingernails. The towel was absolutely crawling with them. Why had nobody noticed them before? Did I still have them after my mother treated me? My father arrived the same evening, fairly angry with my aunt that she had not seen them before. He said he was going to take me immediately to the children's home where my brother was staying.

I was looking forward to it, not having seen my brother since January, nearly four months before. When we arrived, a kind lady called for him, and I was so happy to see him again. But he had stubble on his head, just like my father when he came back from Russia. The lady told us he had lice, and shaving off his hair was the best way to get rid of them. I thought of my own hair and had an idea what was in store for me. My father told me the reason why he had to take Richard away from our grandfather. It turned out that he and his wife ran a thriving business through the black market. His wife was friendly with the British soldiers, who sold her cigarettes, chocolate, tobacco and all kinds of goodies. They were all stored in cases under their single bunk beds, including my brother's. As the deliveries quite often came late in the evenings, my brother never had enough sleep and did not go to school regularly.

The children's home was in a very large villa with a long garden with fruit trees. It was situated at 46 Lokstedter Weg, and there were about 14 children of all ages from toddler to about 11 years old. Most of them were picked up lost and wandering about without their families after the bombings. My brother and I were the exceptions, still having parents. One boy, called Waldemar, who was only eight years old, walked 40 miles (64 kilometres) all the way from Lübeck along the railway lines to Hamburg to look for his uncle, who he knew lived somewhere in the city. There were also three sisters, one of them the eldest in our group.

The lady who ran the home was known as Mutter Bertheau, and the kind looking nurse's name was Marianne Lange. Nurse Marianne took me to a large bathroom. There were rows of washbasins. The first thing she did was to cut off all my hair and put soothing cream onto my raw scalp, which I had been scratching. Then I stripped and had a wash. Nurse Marianne gave me a big long nightdress and showed me to my bunk bed in one of the bedrooms on the first floor. There were three double bunk beds and a single bed in the room. I slept on one of the bottom bunk beds. When all the children were tucked in, she prayed with us. I could not settle down. I was so worried about my head and having to go to school the way I looked. But Nurse Marianne said she was going to give me a woolly hat for school.

The following morning we all had breakfast together in the big dining room downstairs. Mutter Bertheau was sitting at the head of the long table and I was facing her from the other end. She said grace, and we all enjoyed the bread and jam.

I went to school at 41 Erica Strasse. Feeling very conscious about my woolly hat, I felt an outsider and did not like to join in the normal rough and tumble in the playground during breaktimes. The worst thing that happened to me was when a couple of children pulled my hat off and ran away. I was so upset that I ran, covering my head with my hands, to a teacher in the playground. She quickly found the culprits and gave them a telling-off.

I soon settled into the routine at the children's home. We all had to share in the work of keeping the home clean and tidy and followed a rota system. The oldest girls had to make the beds in the mornings before school and help the smaller ones to get washed and dressed. The sheets were washed every four weeks. Every Saturday they had to be turned round a certain way, and by the looks of the seams at the corners we could tell exactly which week it was. A couple of children's and mine had to be washed more often. We were still wetting the beds. I also had to take my turn to polish all the shoes after teatime at the back door – no small task. Another week it was I who had to polish the linoleum on the stairs leading to the first floor, pulling and pushing the heavy polisher to and fro on each step by its big handle. There was also a playroom upstairs, with various toys to play with after school and on Sunday afternoons. We helped with preparing the dinners by peeling potatoes after they were boiled in their skins. Nurse Marianne brought an enormous pot of steaming hot potatoes into the playroom and put it on the table. All the older girls sat around it and peeled them, holding them with a fork in the left hand and peeling them with a small kitchen knife. When we said they were too hot to handle, she used to say: 'Never mind, just be careful, hot potatoes are good against rheumatism.' I also learned how to mend socks, which was a never-ending job with so many children. We did not have many clothes, and the ones we had were soon too small. But the home helped out where it could.

Sundays were always special. We had prayers during weekdays before each meal, but on Sundays Mutter Bertheau read us something appropriate from the Bible and we prayed before we had our breakfast. Occasionally we also went to church on Sundays.

It was great fun when we went with Nurse Marianne to the baker's to collect all the loaves for the home. She gave us rucksacks to carry them in. The customers in the shops always watched us when we were served and must have wondered how we could get through so many loaves. But we were only allowed two slices at a time, as bread was still rationed.

The garden was lovely to play in. There was a swing we all liked very much, and we played hide-and-seek among the fruit trees.

We were both homesick at times, especially my brother, who asked in all his letters to our mother when he could come home again. I felt so upset one day after school that Nurse Marianne sent me to bed. By then I had the nice single bed in our bedroom. I did not want to eat or see anybody. I was still half awake when all the other children came upstairs to get ready for bed. They all gathered around my bed and Nurse Marianne sat down beside me, and they sang a goodnight song and prayed. I felt so much better after that and was all right again the next morning.

The children's home had another large house in Haffkrug at the Baltic Sea, and one day towards the end of June 1946, shortly after the summer holidays started, the oldest children went by car to the main station in Hamburg to catch a train to Lübeck. There we had to wait for two hours to get a connecting train to Haffkrug. Richard celebrated his eighth birthday at the spacious airy home shortly afterwards and was so pleased about his presents. He had a reading book, a skipping rope, colouring book, writing paper, sea shells and a delicious blancmange at dinner. We were very easy to please. We went down to the beach on sunny days, all wearing black swimsuits, and enjoyed splashing around in the clear sea. On the way back we picked wild raspberries along the woodland path. There were four cherry trees in the garden and a swing. The cherries were just ripe on my birthday in July, and I had a big bowlful, which I shared out. The girls hung the double ones on their ears as earrings. Nurse Marianne made me a big birthday cake, and I also had biscuits and a book as presents and a card from my parents and 50 pfennigs.

Only too soon the summer holidays at the Baltic Sea were

over, and we had to come back to the home in Hamburg. But I was looking forward to seeing my father again on his fortnightly visits. He told us that he had found a nicer place for us to live, in Winterhude, another part of Hamburg, which luckily had not seen too much bombing. We were going to have two rooms there in a flat, and there was no black market in that area. But we still had to be patient until our mother came out of hospital. We had not seen her for such a long time. In the meantime it was back to school again. I still wore my woolly hat, because my skin was still sore and had not healed, but my hair had started to grow again. We started to learn the big times-tables, had to write at least two essays weekly and had many spelling tests. I liked school very much now, and the other children respected my woolly hat. We were excluded from school meals now, as we had a good meal each day at the home, but at least twice a week we received some leftover chocolate, which we always looked forward to very much.

Richard and Waldemar became friends. They were over the moon when they were told there was only a one-hour lesson each day when they went back to school in September. So they spent a long time after school in the playground's sandpit and came back home quite dirty. There was still a shortage of teachers and facilities, but things were improving all the time. Much to the boys' disappointment it was soon back to normal school lessons.

During the autumn school holidays we went to the zoo in Hamburg, Hagenbek's Tierpark. We had collected acorns by the bagful on our way home from school during the last week before we broke up. Now we were feeding them to the elephants. At first I was a bit scared of their wet trunks. The zoo had asked the schoolchildren of Hamburg to collect acorns for their animals, as food was still scarce. We saw many different animals, had a ride on a fire engine and enjoyed a Punch and Judy show before we had to return home.

My brother fell ill. He had diphtheria and could hardly

breathe. There was no transport available to get him into the hospital in Eppendorf quickly, so Nurse Marianne wrapped him in blankets and put him into a small open cart, and we both pulled him to the hospital that same evening. I was very worried. We visited him the next day but were only allowed to look at him through a glass partition. However, he looked a little better. He desperately wanted to see our mother, which unfortunately was not possible. I felt lonely with all four members of our family staying in different places, but Richard must have felt much worse. Luckily he soon recovered and came out of hospital.

When the days were getting shorter in the autumn we had a lovely custom in Hamburg. Mutter Bertheau organised a *Laternenumzug* (lantern procession) for us children. After tea we all set out in twos, admiring our colourful paper lanterns, which we held on long sticks in front of us. The lanterns swayed slightly with every step, and the burning candles in them flickered. How exciting it was going out in the dark, when normally we would be getting ready for bed. Now and then one of the candles went out, and Nurse Marianne ran to and fro to relight them. At least none of the paper lanterns caught fire in the light evening breeze. We sang some lantern songs partly in *Plattdeutsch* (Low German)* over and over again. I wonder if this custom is still as popular as it was then, 50 years ago.

At the beginning of November my father had some good news when he came to visit us. He told us our mother was coming out of hospital the following week, and we were coming home. We could not wait; I was so excited, but felt sorry in a way leaving my new friends, Mutter Bertheau and Nurse Marianne behind.

---

* Plattdeutsch is not a dialect, but an independent and important language, restricted to the North German counties. Low German is similar to Dutch and sees its revival in daily radio and on some TV programmes. From time to time even parliamentary sessions are held in Low German in Schleswig-Holstein.

5

By the time we saw our mother again it was the middle of November. She looked so pale and delicate. She could not believe how much we had grown in the meantime. We hugged her for a long time and I promised to be good and help her with the housework.

Winterhude, the part of Hamburg where we lived now, was not as devastated as Eilbek, where I had spent the first seven years of my childhood. Semper-Strasse, the road in which my father had found us two rooms in a first-floor flat, had three- and four-storey blocks of flats. The road was lined with lime trees and the occasional horse chestnut. The branches of one lime tree almost touched the window of our front room, which served us as kitchen, dining room, sitting room and also as bedroom for my parents. My brother and I had a long narrow bedroom at the back with two single beds on one side. We shared the bathroom with the landlady, who spent most of her time in the big kitchen or in her nice lounge with a balcony at the front. This also doubled as a bedroom for her. Mrs Rüdiger was a woman in her sixties and must have resented our invasion at the beginning. For us it was the nicest place and area, apart from the children's home, since we came back from Austria.

The biggest park of Hamburg, Stadtpark, was within walking distance, the large lake Aussen-Alster (Outer Alster) was nearby, with the Krugkoppel Bridge across it, and behind our block of flats was the Goldbek Canal. So there were many areas my brother and I could explore. But first of all we had to get used to yet another school.

My school, an elementary school for girls, at the corner of Forsmann-Strasse, was only a two-minute stroll away from 3 Semper-Strasse. I felt very apprehensive when I climbed the broad stairs to the big school door on the third of December 1946. Mr Lehmann, the headmaster, took me to my class on the first floor to meet my form teacher, Mrs Rebaum. Thirty-seven pairs of eyes looked at me as I stood there in front of the class, being introduced by Mrs Rebaum. She gave me a place in the second row at a wooden desk which still had inkwells. All desks and wooden benches were arranged in rows, so we faced the teacher and the large blackboard behind her desk. Still feeling very conscious about my short hair, I wished I would have brought my woolly hat, especially when two girls sitting behind me said they did not like to look at my head. It was still covered in scabs, which were slowly healing. I was very shy and quiet at the beginning, trying to settle in and getting used to my new teachers.

Mrs Rebaum was around 60 years of age and taught us the German language, grammar and spelling, mathematics, geography and music. She had a beautiful contralto voice and played the piano. I joined her choir, and never thought I could reach the high C, but I did. We only had two lady teachers, and both were spinsters, although Mrs Rebaum insisted on being called Mrs. She gave the impression that she had as many rights and choices as men, be it professionally or socially. And that meant quite a lot 50 years ago. She told us that she had been engaged to a soldier during the First World War, but he had been killed. So she had decided to dedicate her life to teaching children. She was a very strict disciplinarian. Now and then one of us girls felt the slap of the wooden ruler on our outstretched hands for disobedience. I still remember the day I tried to work out the answer to a maths question on the blackboard. I just could not do it. Mrs Rebaum was so annoyed that she banged my head on the blackboard and asked me to get my mother. I knew my mother was ill in bed, but I did not have the courage to tell her, so I ran home sobbing. My poor

51

mother got up and dressed, and we both walked slowly to the school. Every now and then we stopped, and my mother tried to get her breath back. The worst part for her was climbing up the broad stairs to the school door and then on to the first floor. With my mother next to me at the blackboard, I confidently tackled the maths question again and got it right.

The other female teacher was Miss Koch, who was very tall and straight, with her grey hair combed back and tied into a bun. She looked an authoritarian, but was quite soft with us, teaching history and religion.

Sometimes, Mrs Rebaum read to us from her special book, which was an alphabetical list of comic surnames that she had collected over the years. We thought that they were hilarious and screamed with laughter.

Christmas time was exciting. We did not expect any presents, but were delighted when our father came home after work carrying a small Christmas tree, which we decorated with some cotton wool and a few tiny candles. We had to be careful and not use too many because of constant power cuts. They were precious possessions we needed for light. We also had an iron stove in the corner of our living room, which served as cooker for our meagre meals, keeping us warm and giving us light with the oven door slightly ajar.

I learned many new Christmas carols at school. I loved singing, and we all sang carols at home too over Christmas. I never stopped admiring my mother's beautiful voice, and she told me that she had belonged to a choir for many years before we were bombed out.

January 1947 brought us snowstorms and freezing cold weather. We did not have much coal. Many people, including my father and his colleagues, decided to raid the coal waggons which were coming into the marshalling yards at Veddel/Hamburg from the coalmining areas of Dortmund. Some men climbed onto the waggons and threw the big lumps of coal down, while everybody else scrambled to fill their sacks. Suddenly whistles were blown by the police, who were rushing down the embankments with their dogs. My father said afterwards that he had never run so fast in his life, getting away with a few pieces of coal.

The weather continued to be very cold in February, and we had more snow. The Goldbek Canal behind our block of houses was frozen solid, much to our delight. After school we loved to go and slide along it. People walked on it going to and from work, and Mrs Rebaum used it as a short cut to her flat on the other side of the canal. People who were lucky enough to have a sledge or a pair of skates had a great time. Most of us children were just happy queuing up to slide along the glassy path we made. But I was not careful; I fell flat on my face, ending up with a terrific nosebleed and feeling giddy. Two girls from my school picked me up and took me home. My mother soon settled me comfortably, and my nosebleed stopped. To this day, however, I have a bump on my nasal bone, a reminder of my misfortune.

By then we were completely out of any sort of fuel, and we burned all our rubbish in the stove. We could not cook anything or keep warm. After school my brother and I went to the Stadtpark to collect fallen twigs in the snow, but they were difficult to burn and smoked a lot. In the end my father decided with a few colleagues and friends to fell a tree somewhere along a road after dark. Unfortunately, it fell across the road, and he had to redirect the few cars which were coming along. It was very hard work to cut the piece of trunk he brought home into manageable sizes for our stove.

Our teacher, Mrs Rebaum, thought of giving us a treat – an outing to the Harburger Berge for tobogganing. These hills on the other side of the river Elbe are also called the Black Hills because of their colouring. I did not have my own sledge, but one of our neighbours downstairs let me borrow one for this exciting day. It was well used and did not look very strong, but I was only a flyweight.

Off we went to the main railway station in Hamburg to catch a train, a steam train in those days, to alight about an hour later at our destination. We walked for a mile or so through the snow, pulling our sledges behind us. The climb to the top of one of the hills was quite steep, walking along a wide path between plantations of Christmas trees, their branches weighed down by thick layers of snow. The air was crisp and sharp, and we all had rosy cheeks and frozen hands. Our mittens were soon covered in snow, which froze into tiny lumps of ice. Two girls who had no sledges asked me repeatedly to give them a ride on my sledge. I doubted if the sledge would hold us all; but against my better judgement we three squeezed onto the sledge and whizzed down the hill. However, before we could reach the hollow at the bottom the sledge groaned, and the low metal-covered runners slowly splayed outwards. That was the end of our tobogganing for that day. We still had plenty of fun with snowball fights. We went home eventually, tired, hungry, wet and frozen. Luckily my father was able to nail the wooden pieces together again, and our neighbour did not mind when I told her of the mishap.

Mrs Rüdiger, our landlady, asked me quite often into her warm kitchen and taught me how to knit socks. The heels were the most tricky part to do, but eventually I produced a pair of socks with different coloured bits of wool. I wished then my old teacher in Austria could have seen my masterpiece. I graduated to knitting gloves, which were very useful in the winter. To keep warm, I wore baggy trousers under my dress and coat. We did not know the word 'fashion' then.

I settled into school nicely and made a friend called Karin. Sometimes I went to her home after school, and we did our homework together. Near her home was a butcher's shop which sometimes sold hot stock made from marrowbones. It was ideal for cooking swedes and some potatoes. Everything was still rationed, and meat was rare. The regular power cuts continued too, and we ate our stew in near darkness, sitting on my parents' bed in front of the stove, keeping its door slightly ajar. My brother and I had no trouble finishing a second helping.

The snow disappeared at last, and soon we had our Easter

break from school. Mrs Rüdiger now and then received a care parcel from America, and my father was kind enough to pick it up for her from a postal depot about half an hour's walk away. After opening it, she let us have a look at the chocolates, tea, coffee and various tins of fruit and peanuts. Our eyes were getting bigger and bigger looking at all this lovely food. What luxuries! She said that my brother and I could have a teaspoon of peanuts each. My parents found that very mean, and my father did not pick up any other parcels for her.

When we came back to school after our Easter holidays in 1947, we started to learn English. I must admit I was just about scraping by at the beginning, but improved eventually to being an average pupil in this then very difficult language for me.

During the summer holidays we played outside most of the time. There was not enough room indoors to play energetic games, and we had to think of our mother, who was still spending some time in bed. We made many friends with the children who lived in the next block of flats and across the street. At the end of our road was a huge roundabout for one of the tram lines which ended there. Some boys took to jumping on and off the trams when they slowed down before they stopped. They were told many times not to play such dangerous games, but they would not listen. One summer day my brother, some friends and I heard about an accident there and rushed along to see what had happened. Children gathered in the shrubbery opposite the roundabout and looked down at a lifeless boy who was about my brother's age. The top of his skull was gone, and there was a lot of blood. He had fallen off the tram and got caught underneath the wheels. We were subdued and thought of his poor parents.

On really hot days we went to the lake in the Stadtpark. There was an open-air swimming pool and lawns for sunbathing. My parents did not have much money, so we never received any pocket money, but our father gave us enough to buy tickets to get into the swimming pool now and then. We enjoyed it tremendously, splashing and playing in the shallow end of the lake. On other days we went to the park to play hide-and-seek with our friends, or just strolled around discovering new areas all the time. We found a crab-apple tree which was laden with small shiny red apples. We picked as many as we could carry home, and our mother was delighted.

The other flat on our floor was occupied by a pleasant older couple, their daughter and a two-year-old grand-daughter. I loved small children and was allowed to take the little girl out in her pushchair because her mother was working. I never found out what had happened to her father.

Soon it was autumn, and once a week after school I had to go for sunlamp treatment as, in common with many children, I was suffering from vitamin deficiency. The sessions were held in a large villa along the Outer Alster. In a big room there was a tent-like construction in which the sunlamps were situated. About a dozen children had to strip and don goggles, enter the tent and stand in a half-circle along the edge to enjoy the warmth of the rays. On dry days I took the little girl with me. She was looked after by some mothers and nurses while I had the treatment. When I came back I always had a slice of bread with jam as a thank-you. I loved their piano and tried to play some simple tunes on it, but I never played very long, knowing that the little girl's grandfather did not feel too well. A few months later I realised that he must have been very ill; we were told he had died of throat cancer. I could not believe it – he was always so kind to me, and suddenly he was not there any more.

On the third floor lived a woman whose legs were covered in dreadful scars. Nosy as always, we asked her what had happened. She told us that she had jumped into a canal during the firestorm in 1943, trying to get away from certain death. Some people rescued her and took her to a hospital, where she spent a long time. Apparently the nurses queued at her bed to take turns to treat her badly burned legs, changing the bandages and often fainting in the process. At least she survived.

Top left: Ursula's mother, aged about four, and Aunt Anita, aged twelve

Top right: Ursula and Richard in Eilbek, Hamburg, December 1939

Left: Ursula and Richard under the balcony of their bedroom at 30b Rossberg, Eilbek, autumn 1942

Left: Ursula's father in a quiet
moment in Russia, May 1943

Below: The Hamburg Meteorological Office (the 'upside
down chest of drawers') before
it was bombed

Left: Ursula and Richard using a huge cast-iron frying pan as a sledge, Austria, December 1943

Below: Ursula and Richard with their mother in Neumarkt, near Salzburg, July 1944

Ursula and
Richard near the
Waller Lake,
Neumarkt,
summer 1944

Ursula and Richard in
front of their school in
Neumarkt, 1944

Ursula outside the
Neumarkt school, 1944

Tante Höller, the
Kaedings' landlady,
collecting fir cones for
fuel near Neumarkt,
autumn 1944

Left: the school at Neumarkt and the church where Richard decided to ring the bell

Below: Ursula and Richard enjoying an unexpected lift after buying buttermilk at the dairy, Austria 1944

Ursula, her friend Karin, two other pupils and their teacher, Mrs Rebaum, Winterhude, Hamburg, 1948

Ursula and Richard in Semper-Strasse, their home in Winterhude, Hamburg, 1948

Ursula and her father at the allotment, June 1949

Ursula and her family: husband Fred and daughters Jennie (23) and Martina (16)

One evening my father came home from work and told us that he was able to get an allotment next to the airport in Hamburg. The Meteorological Office, where he worked, had some land there to measure wind speeds, temperatures, rainfall etc. They also kept weather balloons in a big shed. We were all excited. It meant that our father could grow vegetables and fruit the following year. One huge field was going to be divided between him and his colleagues, who were all interested.

My father told us that he had worked on a farm as a young man, after he left school. My grandfather had a corner shop which was flourishing. His third wife, however, took too much money out of the business for her own children and herself, and it went downhill. Therefore there was no money left for my father and his two brothers and one sister – born in 1905, he was the youngest of the four. Times were hard in the twenties, and he found a job as a farmhand.

This experience certainly helped when he started on our allotment, and that autumn he spent every Sunday digging it over. The enormous field looked like a construction site, and my brother and I enjoyed going with him. All his colleagues were there, laden with spades and buckets full of horse manure. During the week my brother and I chased after every carthorse in our road, picking up the precious droppings. It was hard work for my father, but eventually our allotment looked all neatly dug into smaller squares surrounded by narrow pathways. He planted a long hedge with cuttings of privet as a windbreak and a long row of raspberry canes, and he was going to build a table and bench in front of it the following spring. About 50 metres away gurgled the Tarpenbek, a stream which my brother and I just managed to jump across. This was our water supply, and we must have carried thousands of gallons from it over the following years. On the other side above the embankment a high fence ran along the perimeter of the airport.

After school we had great fun playing outdoors. All the leaves of the numerous lime and horse chestnut trees were falling, and we collected some beautifully coloured ones for our art classes.

Some children taught us how to fill an empty tin with dried leaves, close the lid up again and make numerous holes at both ends with an old screwdriver, then tie a long piece of string through a couple of them. That way we were able to spin the tin about right over our heads, after we had set fire to the leaves. The escaping smoke made us choke, but we were all competing with each other finding out who could make the biggest smoke patterns.

Another game we loved to play in groups was *Kippel-Kappel*. We took it in turns to hit a small piece of cylindrical wood which was pointed at both ends, roughly 12 centimetres in length and 3–4 centimetres in diameter. We had to lay it across a little trench in the ground and, throwing it up with a wooden stick, try to hit it in the air at the pointed ends. We gained points and took it in turns.

Messerstechen (knife-stabbing) was another of our games. This sounds very dangerous, but consisted of throwing an old blunt kitchen knife exactly onto a line drawn in the soft ground. Again we took it in turns and collected points for the closest hits.

Geschichtenball (story-ball) was a game especially for girls, and we played it at school. All we needed was a wall. One of us started juggling two balls against the wall and inventing a story. As soon as we dropped one of the balls, it was the next girl's turn to tell another story. When it was our second turn we just carried on with our story, and quite often we had up to six different stories going, trying not to get them all muddled up.

Despite the lack of toys, we had a great time playing these inventive games. It also taught us to get on with each other and make up again after quarrels.

Always on the outlook to increase our food intake, we collected bags of beechnuts in the Stadtpark. My mother used them for making cakes, we ate a lot and took the rest to school. Along the Outer Alster on my way to the sunlamp treatment, I saw shrubs growing, some of them laden with sloes. I did not mind their acidity. There were blackberries too, and by the time I reached the villa, I had the feeling I had eaten too many of them.

Autumn was also fungi time. One Sunday my father and one of his colleagues went by train to the Harburger Berge. We were amazed when he came home in the evening carrying a large sackful of beautiful wild mushrooms, *Boletus aereus,* with shiny dark brown caps. We ate quite a few, fried with a couple of onions, that evening. The next day my mother cooked mushroom soup. My brother and I strung the rest of the wiped-clean mushrooms onto long pieces of string after school. When my father came home after work, and after we had finished our mushroom soup, we helped him to put the strings up under the ceiling of our bedroom for drying. Richard and I lay in our beds, looked up and, instead of counting sheep, counted mushrooms until we dropped off to sleep. Even today, I can still smell their earthy odour.

My father also went by *Hochbahn* (elevated train) to the outskirts of Hamburg with a rucksack to ask farmers for potatoes or anything else edible. He walked for miles and came home with only a few pounds of potatoes. He did not have anything to barter with. Some people who did not lose their homes and belongings had the advantage over us and plenty to exchange. In the evening my father told us it looked like a mass migration into the countryside that Sunday. Everybody tried to gather some food to feed the hungry mouths back home. The farmers must have been overwhelmed, and some took full advantage of it. I have been told of Persian carpets in pigsties, which I cannot quite believe.

At school we started getting meals from some very kind-hearted Quakers who tried to feed the needy. One part of the school cellar was set aside for these supplies. Mrs Rebaum personally ladled the soups out from a huge aluminium pot into our metal bowls or billycans. I loved the *Keksmehl-Suppe* (biscuit crumb soup). It was thick and sweet. We also had soup made from chocolate or semolina. The pea soup was another favourite of mine. Occasionally there was enough left for a second helping.

At the beginning of 1948, I fell ill with pleurisy. I had to remain in bed and stay warm. My mother let me stay in my father's bed while he was at work, and I enjoyed being looked after by her. But she was still not too well, and quite often went back to bed when my father had left for work and my brother for school. There was not much to do. We had no radio, nor any books or newspapers to read, so we talked a lot when we felt like it, or dozed. The two little story books I had were nearly falling apart from being read so much, and I knew them backwards. It took a whole month to get better and go back to school. My next report at Easter time was therefore worse.

From March 1948 my father spent every Sunday on our allotment. Richard and I went with him as there was so much sowing and hoeing to do. My father had acquired a spade, a rake and a watering can, which we kept in the balloon shed. He showed us how to put the seeds for carrots, radishes and salad into the furrows he had made and measured out carefully with the help of string. Every time we came to the allotment we ran to our rows of seeds and were amazed how quickly the tiny shoots grew into healthy plants. They soon needed thinning out.

He planted potatoes in long rows when it grew warmer, and various beans, like runner, French, broad and wax. We had a couple of rows of peas too. He also grew tobacco plants in one field. Tobacco was still rationed, and my father liked his pipe. A large plot was set aside for poppies. The seeds were ideal for poppy-cakes, and the surplus of everything could be used for bartering. He did not forget the flowers, including some beautiful sweet peas. When we were having our sandwiches at lunchtime on the bench he had made, the scent of those beautiful sweet peas wafted around in the early summer breeze. I really enjoyed being out at the allotment, even if it meant doing the weeding occasionally and carrying buckets of water from the little stream for the ever-thirsty plants. When the days grew longer my father went during the week after work as well. On Saturdays he only worked until lunchtime, and it was worth going back for more weeding and tending the plants. Geese foraged along the banks of the stream, and parts of the grass were getting quite messy from all their droppings. It meant, however, another good supply of fertilizer, though it was a little bit tricky for my brother and myself to collect.

I loved to lie in the grass watching the skylarks above singing non-stop. For me it was a little piece of heaven, a nature reserve with no disturbance except the occasional noise of an aeroplane. I watched the grasshoppers in the tall grasses, and the bees busy collecting nectar from various wild flowers. There were forget-me-nots, marsh marigolds, yellow flags, buttercups, speedwells and bellflowers, to name but a few. Dragonflies with their transparent veined wings and blue and black or green slender bodies darted along the water, trying to catch small insects. I loved the damselflies, which were slightly smaller, and the blue blotch on each of their gauzy wings shimmered in the sunlight.

Horses grazed near the balloon shed. They were very sociable animals and came along to nuzzle us, hoping for a carrot or two. There were mushrooms shooting out of the ground overnight, and we collected them as soon as we entered the fenced-in area through a gate.

Life would have been perfect if my mother could have come with us on Sundays to see the allotment, especially now everything was growing and flowering so well. My father had built a wooden table by now, and behind the bench the raspberries were ripening. We had to walk quite a long distance to the tram stop, and at the other end it was about a mile to reach the allotments. My mother unfortunately only managed to walk a couple of hundred metres to cross a bridge over the Goldbek canal and was completely puffed out and could not get her breath back. I felt so sorry for her and offered to stay behind with her; but she insisted on my going with my father and my brother to the allotment, while she slowly walked back home again. The whole day I worried how she was. My father said it was such a pity, but there were no taxis then, as far as I knew, and my father could not have afforded one, anyway.

In the middle of June 1948 the Western Allies unveiled the Deutschmark, to replace the Reichsmark in West Germany. Everybody was only allowed to exchange 40.00 Reichmarks for 40.00 Deutschmarks. I will never forget the shop windows the following morning. They were bursting with food we had not seen for years, including bananas and oranges in the greengrocer's window. The only orange I ever had was given to me by an American officer in Austria, and I could not remember ever having seen bananas before. Now we had all the goods in the shops and not enough money to buy them; we had to be careful with our money for it to last us until my father came home with the next monthly pay packet.

At the same time the Russian blockade in Berlin went on, and the Western Allies tried to beat it with round-the-clock airlifts by Dakota aircraft, which took off from an air base near Hanover and landed at Gatow in the British zone of the city. The Russians had banned all food supplies by road from the Soviet areas which surrounded Berlin – Berliners called themselves *Insulaner* (islanders). The city itself was divided into four zones, occupied separately by the British, Americans, French and Russians.

During the summer holidays I learned to swim at the open-air swimming pool in the Stadtpark. I went nearly every day for lessons, and was proud when I eventually managed 100 metres in the deep pool. I begged my father to come and watch me, and one morning at six thirty, I was in the pool, with him and the instructor watching me. I just followed the long pole the instructor held in front of me, in case I needed assistance, I earned my certificate that day, swimming the required distance. However, I never received it, as it cost 50 pfennigs and I did not like to ask my father for the money. He went straight to work afterwards, starting at 8.00 a.m.

By then we had our first home-grown vegetables. We ate many of them raw, like the carrots, after we had pulled them out of the ground and wiped the dirt off. The peas were sweet and I even ate the yellow wax beans raw. There was a big surplus of runner beans. We all sat around our small table in the living room and cut piles of them into tiny slivers. They were then put into a wooden barrel with plenty of salt, and kept in our cellar. Before we could use them the following winter, they had to be rinsed a few times. They were still quite salty when we eventually cooked and ate them. Our cellar was not very big, but there was enough space for a big wooden box which eventually was filled up with our home-grown potatoes. My father carried them home sack by sack from the allotment. He was really working hard; he also dug a couple of clamps in the ground for the carrots and a huge pile of swedes, which we took to school in raw slices during the winter months when there was not enough bread. He still went to the allotment now and then during the winter to collect more swedes, Brussels sprouts, red and white cabbage, and also kale, which grew to enormous size next to the compost heap. We collected the last dried runner beans, put some aside for planting the next spring and put the rest in a large storage jar for cooking.

Small potatoes were stored in baskets under our bunk beds. We had a little rectangular window in our bedroom, into which a Virginia creeper with its long tendrils forced its way. The outside walls of the block of flats were covered with it. In the autumn the leaves turned a spectacular crimson. We looked down onto a run that one of the tenants had built for his dozen or so chickens. My brother and I were little devils at times and tried to pelt the chickens with tiny potatoes through the wire mesh. Fortunately we never hit them, but they scattered when one of these missiles dropped through a hole in the netting. Our neighbour downstairs never said anything, and probably was delighted about the extra food. Our mother always wondered why those potatoes were getting depleted.

Now we had plenty of vegetables to see us through the winter, but one thing we were always short of was meat. One idea crossed my father's mind; but I will come back to that later on.

There was a problem to be solved about the hundreds of tobacco leaves which needed picking and drying. It was a very sticky and messy job for us. After bringing the first batch home, my brother and I threaded the leaves onto strings. Our hands were black with the juices. Like the wild mushrooms the previous autumn, we dried the tobacco leaves under the ceiling of our bedroom. Once they were dry, my father very carefully piled them into small stacks, dribbled various essences onto them, tied them with string into parcels and stored them in shoe boxes. After a few weeks he checked them and was quite pleased with the result. With a sharp knife, he then cut the parcels into narrow strips, and the tobacco was ready to be smoked in his pipe. But I did not like the smell of it very much. It reminded me of the dried weeds and yellowed potato plants we burned in big piles on our allotment. Still, the potatoes we cooked in the hot ashes afterwards were delicious.

My cousin Lotte had returned from the Land Army a couple of years before and now worked for a chemist, delivering medicines to various patients. She had just acquired a second-hand car, a 1936 Opel Olympia, with built-in lights, and offered to drive my brother and me around the block. This was a treat, sitting in a car. I was amused by the little red indicators which popped up like arrows when we drove around the corners.

More excitement was to come. One of the greatest occasions in Hamburg is the *Hamburger Dom,* the *'Volksfest'* of the North. It attracts people by the thousand from all the surrounding counties and Hamburg itself. It is a large fair, held on the Heiligengeistfeld (Holy Ghost Field) near the Reeperbahn in St Pauli. The name 'Dom' is derived from a medieval Christmas market which was held in a hall called Schappendom, part of the eleventh-century St Marien Cathedral. Unfortunately, the cathedral was beyond repair at the beginning of the nineteenth century and had to be demolished.

The Hamburger Dom takes place from the beginning of November well into December and is also held in spring and summer. Huge fireworks light up the skies in the evenings.

Lotte treated us to an evening out at the Christmas fair and picked us up in her car. We were overwhelmed by the noise and the illuminations everywhere. Irresistible smells of roasted almonds, doughnuts, grilled sausages and liquorice surrounded us, and Lotte bought us a couple of sausages and doughnuts. We went on the ghost train, being smothered in cobwebs and nearly touching a skeleton with its rattling bones. The caterpillar, the waltz train and the chairoplane were my favourite rides. Lotte was shocked when she counted the cost afterwards. Twenty Deutschmarks was a lot of money, but she said: 'It is only money, and I am happy you loved it so much.' We did not stop talking about it when we arrived back home until my mother said that we were well past our bedtime.

When I went to school, it was the custom at Christmas to hold a Yule Club. It meant putting all our names into a hat and each of us drawing one out. Then we would bring a present for that person. I remember pulling Mrs Rebaum's name out and wondering what sort of present I could give her for Christmas. My father came to my rescue and gave me a pack of writing paper and envelopes, still a rarity, which I wrapped up and tied with a big ribbon. On our last school day before the Christmas holidays we brought our presents in and piled them up along the floor under the blackboard. We took it in turns to come forward, picking one up and calling out the name. There was a lot of guessing going on about who we had received our presents from when we unwrapped them at our desks. It was very unusual picking out one's own name from the hat; but it happened to me. I received a beautiful bone china cup and saucer filled with chocolates tied up with a large red ribbon. My guess was my teacher, and she admitted that it was her when I asked. I thanked her very much for such a lovely present. Then our teacher lit all four candles on the huge advent wreath which hung from the ceiling of our classroom and we sang Christmas carols.

We also sang carols during the weeks leading up to Christmas at several nursing homes, this time with a very much smaller number in our choir. We were about a dozen, including me. I remember the old ladies sitting in their armchairs listening to us and smiling happily. At the entrance of the room stood a large sack with biscuits, and as we filed out through the door, we were allowed one biscuit each. Only one – I could have eaten many more!

6

In the spring of 1949, because of the shortage of meat, my father decided to buy a lamb from a market in Ochsenzoll, a small place then, to the north of the airport. Richard and I fell in love with the soft and forever bleating lamb. We had to walk for miles along the country lanes, holding on to a long thin rope we had put around the neck of Lotte. (I do not know what my cousin thought about our calling the lamb after her.) The poor animal seemed very tired after a couple of miles, stopping now and then to nibble at the grass verges, and my father thought of a way to carry it to our allotment. He knocked on a farmhouse door and asked if we could borrow a cart. The farmer was very obliging and let us have one which could have carried an ox. Lotte rested on it, and we three had to pull the cart the rest of the way to our allotment. My father must have been really tired out that evening, pulling the cart back to the farmhouse and walking to the allotment afterwards.

In the meantime, Richard and I tried to build a stable with wooden planks in one corner of the balloon shed and put plenty of straw in it. He was quite pleased with our efforts, but had to adjust the planks and nail them together for more stability. One of his colleagues, who had retired in the meantime, offered to put the lamb out every morning when he came to the allotment.

A few weeks later another colleague acquired a lamb as well, which his son called Liesel. There was plenty of space in the balloon shed to enlarge our stable. At least they had each other for company. It meant, of course, finding food for them for the evenings when my father and his colleague took it in turns after work to take them into the shed from their grazing place. Richard and I went up and down the stairs of the blocks of flats to knock on doors to ask for vegetable scraps. All our neighbours soon knew us and saved their leftovers. Lotte and Liesel put on weight and grew fast. Whenever we went to the allotments, we played with them. We grew very fond of them and could not imagine them being slaughtered at Christmas time so that we could have plenty of meat. I told my father I was not going to touch anything, and when the butcher came to end Lotte's and Liesel's lives, I ran down to the little stream crying about the loss of my pet. But hunger eventually got the better of me. The delicious smell of roasted lamb wafted through the flat, and when it was dinner time, I ate the meat my mother had put on my plate, although I felt very guilty. Most of the meat was bottled afterwards for leaner times during the winter months.

After Easter during the same year I started going to confirmation lessons once a week in the evenings. The Matthäus Kirche was about a mile away from our lodgings, and I walked to it with two girls from my class.

Pastor Knuth was a very kind man, and I knew many passages of the Bible and hymns by heart from my time in the children's home.

Spring was a beautiful time. The lime trees in our road were green again, the horse chestnut trees were in blossom, which reminded me of the erect wax candles on our last Christmas tree, and I was looking forward to going to our allotment once more. I learned to ride a bicycle – not my own, but one belonging to a boy in our circle of playmates. One of the children let me borrow an odd pair of old roller skates. I had to tie them to my shoes with string, and off I went on the traffic-free asphalt road next to the Goldbek canal. With blue skies and the sun shining, all the children came out of their flats to have a go on their roller skates, riding their bikes or play hide-and-seek.

One afternoon I heard some music and singing nearby.

When I looked out of our small bedroom window, I saw a man in the Hinterhof, playing a violin and his wife, I assumed, singing. The music from the Vienna Woods sounded beautiful and somehow sad. It struck a strange chord in me, and I wondered what else there was in the world outside my familiar surroundings.

One evening my father came home with a little second-hand radio. At last my mother could listen to the NDR (Norddeutscher Rundfunk) in her lonely time, when we took off for the allotment at weekends. I was intrigued how we could receive the programme through the air and tried to find other stations by twiddling the knobs; but all I could hear were hissing and grumbling noises, which I thought were coming straight from the atmosphere miles above us.

At school we learned all about astronomy, and Mrs Rebaum took our class twice that year to the planetarium in the Stadtpark. My interest was awakened, and my father borrowed some books from the Meteorological Office about constellations, faraway planets and cloud formations. He also wrote down a list of the highest mountains and longest rivers of the world, which I still treasure, because of my dreadful mark in geography in my last Easter school report. He was very pleased when my autumn report showed a great improvement.

One episode I still remember so well, it could have happened yesterday. One beautiful summer evening my father took me to watch my first big firework display at the Outer Alster. Crowds lined the embankments, and it must have been embarrassing for my father when I kept calling out all the time: 'Look, Dad! Have you seen this one? Isn't it beautiful? Look at these colours!'

Mrs Rebaum decided we should give a concert with our choir the following February. This meant having extra music lessons after school, when she taught us many beautiful old folk songs. The proceeds of those two choir concerts were going towards a school holiday the following August. We decided to design our own tickets. During art lessons we were busy cutting out coloured cards, painting flower garlands and writing the dates and times of the concert onto them. They were only 30 pfennigs each, and we had no problem selling them, filling the hall of another school nearby to bursting point. Unfortunately, my mother could not come due to her illness, but my father and brother came on the first evening. We all wore black skirts and white blouses, and on our heads were home-made garlands of pink and white daisies, intertwined with green leaves from a flower shop. We marched in single file through the audience along the aisle to the stage, singing: '*Konzert ist heute angesagt im frischen grünen Wald*' (A concert is announced today in the fresh, green woods). Mrs Rebaum played the Steinway piano to accompany us. She also sang a few Lieder by Brahms. It was a success, I believe. People were happy coming out one evening to enjoy themselves, and not just thinking about where to get the next meal from.

Things were improving slightly. We were still poor, but there was more food available now. The allotment helped greatly; my father worked non-stop every available hour he had to spare. There was no shortage of vegetables and fruit. We had red- and blackcurrants and gooseberries, our raspberry hedge behind the bench grew bigger each year, and we had our first crop of strawberries. There was a butcher's shop in our area which sold horsemeat. It seemed to be in bigger supply than any other sort of meat. I quite liked the smoked sausages, which had a strong and unusual taste, and my mother made a meat loaf occasionally from minced meat. Richard and I usually did the shopping for her after school, because by then she looked very frail and weak and spent most of her time resting.

Mrs Rebaum was busy negotiating with the education board to get our class into the vocational school of the clothing industry for our last school year after the Easter holidays in 1950. Every year then, one class of girls in Hamburg was chosen to spend the last school year there to acquire some practical tuition. Our teacher was lucky to get us in. It meant walking a long distance for nearly an hour to

Uferstrasse, another district in Hamburg, and then back again.
How different this year was going to be. We were taught how to use the sewing machine, producing a white apron with many different stitches. Embroidery was another subject. I liked designing my own patterns of cross stitch for a square tablecloth. The trickiest subject for me was modelling heads of papier mâché. We built up layer upon layer of newspaper and eventually dried them slowly in the ovens of our school kitchen. I decided on a butcher and a policeman. We had to dress them too, which was easy enough for the butcher – I just put him into a white gown. He looked the spitting image of the butcher in the horsemeat shop, with his plump red cheeks. The policeman's uniform was more difficult. In the end I panicked when the puppets had to be handed in the following morning. My poor mother somehow managed to find some scraps of navy blue material, and sat up in bed until midnight to make some trousers, a matching jacket with shiny buttons and a policeman's helmet, while I was fast asleep. I gave her a big hug the following morning for my lovely figure of law and order.

This was not the end of it. We had to invent stories after building a puppet stage, and act them out. I hated it, always being very shy; but somehow I survived the ordeal.

We learned cooking, and ate our meals after the lessons. My unfortunate family had to try my concoctions on some evenings. When my father said one evening he would prefer a piece of meat to my thin vanilla soup with semolina dumplings, I gave up.

We also learned folk dancing. The only trouble was not having any boys in our class, so every other girl had to dress up as a boy with lederhosen. I had to borrow my costume, a dirndl dress, from Karin, my best friend, when we invited the parents one evening to our performance. Poetry was another of our subjects, and I had to recite a poem with two other girls on stage, taking it in turns with the verses. I was nervous and suffered from stage fright. When it was my turn, my mind went absolutely blank after the first two lines. I stood there wanting to sink into the ground, with everybody

71

in the school hall looking at me. It seemed ages before the girl next to me whispered the next word, and I carried on with the rest of the verse. My teacher never said anything afterwards. She must have sensed my dilemma. We also sang some folk songs, and the parents admired our handicrafts in our classroom.

One day after school four classmates and I turned a corner on the way home, and a man exposed himself to us. Two girls had fits of giggles, but the rest of us found it very embarrassing. We ended up at the police station at the Carl-Muck-Platz in the city a couple of days later, after telling our teacher about it the following day. There we looked through piles of photo albums to find the culprit; but he was never caught.

We were looking forward to our fortnight's holiday on the largest island in the North Sea, Sylt, during our school holidays in August. Just the train journey was exciting. It was not far short of four years since December 1946, when we became a family again, and the first time one of us was going away on a holiday. I felt guilty in a way leaving everybody behind, especially my mother, who could have done with a holiday most of all. My father had to pay about 30 Deutschmarks towards it. The rest had been raised from our concerts.

We stayed at the 5-City-Holiday Camp in List, the most northern place on the island. We were surrounded by sand dunes, through which we had to find our way to the beach. The sea air gave us big appetites, and we ate large portions of the meals in the dining hall at the first of two sittings. Our rooms had bunk beds and washbasins. On the window sills we dried starfish, which we had to throw out eventually because they stank so much, poor things! We collected piles of beautiful shells on the wide sandy beach, went for long walks around the top of the island, and wrestled with the sometimes rough waves. Some days it was quite cold and very windy, even though it was supposed to be the height of summer; but it did not deter us from plunging into the sea. My teacher never thought I would last out so long in the cold water, as I was still very skinny. But the waves made us forget the cold, and we enjoyed the sea tremendously. After the evening meals we played board games in the dining hall. Somebody played an accordion and we sang songs. We were never too late in bed – the sea air made us very tired.

I wrote a couple of postcards to my parents, wondering how my mother was, not having heard from her. Most girls had letters from home, and I worried. Eventually I received a postcard from her in the second week, and all seemed to be well.

Everyone was sad when the last day arrived and we had to pack our little suitcases. But once we had boarded the train, we were excited about seeing our families again. There was so much to tell. My father waited on one of the platforms at the main station in Hamburg, among all the other parents. He was pleased to see me again, but was unusually quiet and distant. When we arrived back home in our lodgings, I found out why. My mother was ill in bed, looking very pale, and her breathing seemed difficult. The contrast to my suntan was enormous, and I felt ashamed somehow that I was so bubbly, wanting to tell her everything about the holiday at once.

Soon it was back to school. When I arrived home in the early afternoons I started on the housework, not that there was an awful lot to do, keeping just two rooms clean; but the washing was the main problem. Everything had to be washed by hand. Nobody had heard of washing machines then. Luckily, the bed linen went to a laundry nearby. But there was still plenty of coloured washing left for me to do. I used a washboard in the oval zinc bath which stood on a large wooden stool next to my mother's bed. The steam of the hot soapy water drifted to the ceiling, and the smell of green soap and dirty washing was not the most pleasant one for my mother to breathe in. While I was busy rubbing the last dark hand towel clean, my mother asked me to stop, but I said: 'This is the last piece. I will just finish this.' Thinking back now, I wonder if she just wanted to talk to me for a little while; but then the precious moment was gone.

The next day, a Thursday in November, my mother went into hospital. In the afternoon ambulance men came upstairs with a stretcher and carried her away. Richard and I looked on and waved when the ambulance pulled away. I felt absolutely deserted, and with my arms around my brother's shoulders we slowly climbed up the stairs to our empty lodgings. We were sitting at the small table in front of the window, looking out for our father coming home. Eventually we saw him walking down the road very slowly, as if he was carrying a heavy burden on his shoulders. He told us that our mother was very ill, and that we would go and visit her the following Sunday. The hospital was not too far away, near Mundsburg, and we could reach it by tram in less than half an hour.

The Marien-Krankenhaus was a Roman Catholic hospital and when we arrived on Sunday afternoon, we saw nuns in their habits rushing about quietly. The whole atmosphere was tranquil and reassuring. We found our mother lying in a bed next to a large window. Her breathing was very shallow, and now and then she had to use a spittoon. I found it quite awful and promised to bring her some handkerchiefs on our next visit the following Wednesday. I could come straight after school, which was only a 15-minute walk away. Our father also offered to bring some oranges next time. But there was not going to be a next time.

The following Monday my father went to work, and Richard and I to school, at 8.00 a.m., the usual time. I had a terrible cold. No wonder; November is always a misty and wet month in Hamburg. At around 9.30 a.m. the head-mistress knocked on our classroom door and had a word with Mrs Rebaum, then asked me to come to the office with her. My father was there, sitting slumped in a chair, looking ashen.

I only took one look at him and knew instantly that something dreadful had happened to my mother. He had come to take me home. I went back to the classroom to collect my bag. Nobody talked; it was very quiet, and

74

everybody looked subdued. Mrs Rebaum must have told the class what had happened. My father and I walked to the tram stop. He kept saying: 'They did not let me see her, they did not let me see her! She suffocated, she suffocated! She is – was – only forty!' But what could I do? Sitting on a wooden bench on the tram, I kept saying to him that it was better that way, she had suffered so much the last years. Then he said in a very small voice: 'If only I had brought her the oranges yesterday.' We kept looking out of the window as the tram trundled along, so as not to show our faces to the other passengers.

When we arrived home, Aunt Else was there preparing some lunch. My father went back to work afterwards, and to arrange everything for the funeral. When Richard came home from school, he wondered why I was already home, and why Aunt Else was there, too. He kept asking: 'What is wrong? What is the matter? Why is Aunt Else here?' My aunt did not say anything, so I had to tell Richard: *'Mutti ist tot!'* (Mum is dead). He sobbed bitterly.

The Ohlsdorfer Friedhof is, next to the central cemetery in Chicago, the biggest one in the world, and also the largest park in Hamburg.

On the day of the funeral all our relatives and many of my father's colleagues, my teachers, including Herr Lohmann, my headmaster, my schoolfriends and our neighbours were sitting in the chapel of the crematorium to pay their last respects to my mother. There stood my mother's coffin, bedecked in flowers, and next to it Pastor Knuth, my confirmation teacher, preaching. Of all the music I heard being played, *Ave Maria,* my mother's favourite song, stood out. Suddenly it hit me, my mother was never coming back. I cried and sobbed my heart out during the rest of the service. I just could not stop myself. At that moment I realised my childhood was over for ever.

75

EPILOGUE

World War Two caused a great deal of damage to Hamburg. Although some parts escaped more or less intact, others, especially where the firestorm occurred, were devastated. After the war, the city was slowly rebuilt. The thousands of Nissen huts built as temporary accommodation in the parks and on the outskirts of the city eventually disappeared. Today, Hamburg is once again a vibrant city with its gates open to the world.

I met my future husband, Fred, on holiday in Spain in 1967 and we married in Canterbury in August 1970. We settled in Sittingbourne, Kent and have two daughters – Jennifer was born in 1972, Martina in 1979.

My father remarried in 1951 and died of cancer shortly after my wedding.

My brother, Richard, is a banker and works in Düsseldorf. He and his wife, Marlis, have a son, Patrick, who is studying ship design at the University of Hamburg.

My aunts, Else Lütje and Anita Friese, and my uncle, Fiete Kaeding, died in their eighties. Tante Else's husband, Willi, died of cancer in the 1970s, shortly after his retirement.

Cousin Lotte married a miner and they now live in retirement near Dortmund. They have a son, Volker.

Lotte's sister, Erika, died aged 13 of a heart defect.

I never saw Tante Höller or Oma Dachgruber again. During a visit to Neumarkt in 1978, Richard visited the shop which is owned by a descendant of Tante Höller.

The war caused untold suffering, hardship and disruption all over Europe. The fight against tyranny resulted in millions of deaths but paved the way for the post-war years of peace and reconciliation. However, it is regrettable that not all of Europe has experienced the freedom and prosperity that most western Europeans have enjoyed.

APPENDIX

I still have the letters that Richard and I wrote to our mother between July and November 1946, from Hamburg and from the Haffkrug Children's Home, during her illness.

Several were written on notepads which reflected the times in which they were produced, having appropriate slogans at the bottom.

4 July 1946

Dear Mummy,

I am very well. Richard has his blue knitted trousers here. We are in Haffkrug where it is very beautiful. There are other children with us. We have been on the beach a few times already. There is a nice playground in Haffkrug. Today we put our swimsuits on. It is such nice weather. In the playground is a swing. I am glad that we have a new home[1]. Richard's birthday was very nice. He has received quite a few presents. Nearly every time we go on to the beach, we collect seashells. You can play very nicely with seashells. My birthday is soon as well.[2] I am looking forward to it. Many greetings to you

Your dear Ursula

[1] Two rooms in a flat.
[2] 18 July.

4 July 1946

Dear Mummy,

Mummy, I would like to come home again. Perhaps you can come home to Daddy in two or three weeks. Mummy, we have gone to Haffkrug[1]. There it is very nice, even nicer than in Hamburg. Mummy, first we drove by car to the main railway station in Hamburg. Then we went by train to Lübeck. There we had to wait for two hours, and then we went at 2 p.m. by train to Haffkrug. Mummy, my birthday[2] was really nice. Mummy, I got a story book and a skipping rope, and writing paper, a colouring book and seashells, and a nice pudding. All that I have received. Many greetings from

your dear Richard

---

[1] A summer children's home on the Baltic Sea.
[2] 27 June.

(From the children's home, 4 July 1946)

Dear Mrs Kaeding,

Both your children are keeping well. Here in the summer home they are enjoying themselves and are cheerful. As far as we can, we help out with the clothing from the home. Hopefully you are feeling better again now. I would wish this for you so much. With kind greetings,

Nurse Marianne Lange
Children's Home
Haffkrug

21.7.1946

Dear Mummy,

I thank you for your dear letter. Saturday we have been to the beach. There was a low tide. Sometimes we pick wild raspberries. Mummy, Ursula's birthday was very nice. Mummy, we are coming home soon, aren't we? And Ursula was very pleased about the 50 pfennigs. Many greetings from

your dear Richard

21.7.1946

Dear Mummy,

I thank you for your dear letter. It was very nice on my birthday. On a birthday table I saw a gateau and many biscuits. Also cherries for me, a book, a birthday card and a picture. Mummy, I only corrected a few mistakes in Richard's letter. We live very close to a wood. Often we pick wild raspberries, and the blackberries will also soon be ripe. There are four cherry trees here. On 20 July we swam in the sea. It was low tide. There I saw seagulls. We also get lovely food here. Dear Mummy, couldn't we write to Tante Höller[1] once? Many thousand greetings from

your dear Ursula

---

[1] In Austria.

Den 21. 7. 1946.

Liebe Mutti!

Ich danke Dir für deinen lieben Brief.
An meinen Geburtstag war es sehr
schön. Ich sah auf einem Geburts-
tagstisch eine Torte und viele Plätzchen,
Auch Kirschen für mich, ein Buch, eine
Karte und ein Bild. Mutti, ich habe
Richard nur ein paar Fehler verbes-
sert. Wir wohnen dicht an einem
Wald. Auch pflücken wir oft Him-
beeren und die Brommbeeren werden
auch bald reif. Vier Kirschbäume
sind hier. Den 20. Juli haben wir auch
gebadet. Es war Eppe. Da hab ich Mö-
wen gesehen. Auch kriegen wir hier viel
schönes Essen. Liebe Mutti können wir
nicht einmal an Tante Höller schrei-
ben? Viele tausend Grüße sendet Dir

Deine liebe Ursula

Liebe Mutti!

Wie geht es Dir? Mir geht es sehr gut. Papa war am Sonnabend hier und hat uns besucht. Sage Papa wenn er zu Dir auf Besuch kommt, daß ich ein Kleid brauche. Ich habe drei Kleider hier. Das gestrickte blaue Kleid, das ist zu warm. Richard und ich sind wieder am Lockstedterweg. Ich gehe noch gerne zur Schule. Wie wir noch nicht in Haffkrug waren, sind wir einmal alle zusammen nach Langenhorn Mitte gefahren. Nach der Kirche sind wir gegangen. Da blieben wir bis zum Abend. Wir durften auf den Turm gehen und die Umgebung sehen. Dann aßen wir bei der Kirche auf der Wiese Abendbrot. Viele Grüße sendet Dir

Deine Ursula und Richard

3.9.46

Dear Mummy,

How are you? I am very well. Daddy came on Saturday to visit us. When Daddy comes to visit you, please tell him that I need a dress. I have three dresses here, the blue knitted dress is too warm. Richard and I are back at the Lokstedterweg[1]. I still like going to school. Before we went to Haffkrug, we all went to Langenhorn Mitte[2]. We went to church there. We stayed there until evening. We were allowed to go up the tower to see the surrounding area. Then we had our Abendbrot[3] next to the church on the lawn. Many greetings from

your Ursula and Richard

---

[1] In Hamburg.
[2] Place on the outskirts of Hamburg.
[3] Tea.

(Note at base of pad: *Shorthand today more than ever means small print.*)

7.9.46

Dear Mummy,

Daddy was here yesterday to visit us. Mummy, I like to go to school here. We only have a one hour lesson. Next to the school is a sand pit. When I and a boy, who is called Waldemar, go to school, we play also in the sand pit. Often we play on the swing. Sometimes we also play in the garden.

The Child at the Well

Wet nurse, wet nurse,
The child is awake.
But she is still asleep.
The birds are singing,
The sun is laughing.
On the hill the sheep are grazing.

Wet nurse, wet nurse!
The child gets up,
It ventures further and further.
Down to the well it is running.
There grow flowers and herbs.

Wet nurse, wet nurse,
The well is deep!
She sleeps as if she would lay in the well.
The child runs fast, as it has never run before.
The flowers are becoming enticing from afar.
Now it stands at the well.

Now it is at the destination.
Now it picks the flowers with pleasure,
But soon it is tired of the game,
It looks down into the depth.[1]

Your Richard. Get better soon.

---

[1] Richard learnt this poem at school but was unable to complete it as he ran out of paper.

23 September 1946

My dear Mummy,

I am looking forward to coming home. Dear Mummy, how are you? Hopefully better. I am happy that you are being well looked after. Eight days ago Daddy brought me a dress, skirt and blouse. Daddy also wants to have a pair of trousers made for Richard. At school we are already learning the big times tables. Also Daddy brought us each 12 sheets of drawing paper and a maths and writing exercise book. Next time, Daddy says, he will bring us a pencil. Every fortnight Daddy comes to visit. I am very well. I know everything around here. At school we write two essays each week and many dictations. I think, that you cannot offer us that much.[1] Many greetings from

your dear Ursula

---

[1] How I regret this sentence even to this day. It was no wonder that my mother was extremely annoyed and tore this letter up, only for it to be stuck together again by my father. I did not mean to hurt her. After all, I was only ten years old.

23 September 1946

My dear Mama,

I want to come home and wish that you soon come home. I have a new pair of trousers. I have tried them on. But Daddy took them home again. And Daddy visits us every fortnight. And once Daddy brought us each a writing and maths exercise book and 12 sheets of drawing paper.

Your dear Richard

Better improvement[1]

---

[1] This was meant to mean 'Get better soon.

4.10.46

Dear Mummy,

Now are the autumn school holidays, and on

Thursday we went on an excursion to Hagenbeck's Tierpark[1]. There we saw elephants, apes, canaries, llamas, camels, racoons, stalking birds, parrots, deer, stags, rhinoceros, giraffes, storks, emus, kangaroo. Afterwards we had a ride on a fire engine. Then we saw Punch & Judy. Then we went home. Many greetings, your

dear Ursula

Star Journey

And the sun made the long ride around the
world.
And the stars said: 'We travel with you around the
world.'
And the sun told them off: 'You stay at home. I will
burn your golden eyes out on the fiery ride around
the world.'
And the stars went to the dear moon in the night
and said, 'You who are enthroned on the clouds in
the night, let us wander with you because your
mild light will never burn our eyes.'
And he took them, companions of the night.

---

[1] The zoo in Hamburg.

4.10.46

My dear Mummy,

How are you? The day before yesterday we went to the zoo. We went to see the elephants, and we fed them with acorns[1]. And now comes a poem:

There was once a little man
who climbed into a little coffee pot.
Then he climbed out again
and the story is finished.

86

The card, and the teddy and the jumping jack are from Richard. Many greetings from your

dear Richard

---

[1] In those days when food was scarce, children were encouraged to collect acorns with which to feed zoo animals.

20.10.46

Dear Mummy, dear Daddy,

Today Daddy came to visit us. I like it here very much. I gave Daddy my school report. Yesterday we went to a recreation field. There a few girls and I tried to do handstands. The other girls managed to do it, turning it into a flip. But I could not do it. Then we went home.

At school we got chocolate. But only the children who have meals. Many children do not eat meals there. But when there are leftovers, the other children get the rest of the chocolate.

Dear Mummy, I hope that you are soon well again. Many greetings from
your
dear Ursula

The spare paper is for Daddy and you for letter writing.

10.11.46

Dear Mummy,

Dear Mummy, I thank you for your dear letter. You will have a help, and that will be me. I am well. We shall get chocolate here. At school we get chocolate twice a week. Dear Mummy, do not worry about Richard. Dear Mummy, I wish you a

87

good recovery and much luck. Many greetings from
your
dear Ursula

(Note at base of pad: *Save still more paper.*)

Liebe Mutti!

Liebe Mutti ich danke Dir für
Deinen lieben Brief. Du wirst
schon eine Hilfe haben und
daß bin ich. Mir geht es gut.
Wir werden hier auch Schokola-
de bekommen. In der Schule be-
kommen wir zwei mal in der
Woche Schokolade. Liebe Mutti,
mache Dir keine Sorgen über
Richard. Liebe Mutti, ich wünsche
Dir gute Besserung und viel Glück
Viele Grüße sendet Dir
                Deine
                liebe Ursula

Noch mehr Papier sparen!   50

89